SHORT STORY WRITING

by Wilson R. Thornley

Wilson R. Thornley has established a reputation as one of the most successful high school teachers of short story writing in the country. Among the many citations his students have received are awards from The National Scholastic Writing Awards Competition, The Atlantic Creative Writing Contest and publication in Scholastic Magazine, Seventeen and Literary Cavalcade.

SHORT STORY WRITING

WILSON R. THORNLEY

BANTAM BOOKS
TORONTO · NEW YORK · LONDON · SYDNEY

RL 7, IL 9+

SHORT STORY WRITING

A Bantam Book / November 1976
2nd printing ...... August 1977
3rd printing ...... August 1979
4th printing .... September 1981

Bantam Books are published by Bantam Books, Inc. Its trademark, consisting of the words "Bantam Books" and the portrayal of a rooster, is Registered in U.S. Patent and Trademark Office and in other countries. Marca Registrada. Bantam Books, Inc., 666 Fifth Avenue, New York, New York 10103.

PRINTED IN THE UNITED STATES OF AMERICA

13 12 11 10 9 8 7 6 5 4

To My Wife

Contents

PART I

1

Scene in The Short Story

The art of telling stories through dramatic representation seems so old as to be a natural characteristic of the human mind and spirit. We seem naturally to want to communicate experience, and we have an inbred conviction that our experiences are unique and interesting to others. Reporting our experiences releases us from inner tension, socially and psychologically. The report usually takes the form of a sequential story —something we have accomplished, a problem solved, a conquest attained. Telling it provides a kind of catharsis. It bridges the gap between our inner self and the listener.

Everybody tells stories: the counselor or psychologist illustrates a point or gains rapport with a story; the physician relates a case history; the businessman cites examples, and so on. In school, the student writes narrative themes. These naturally require careful structuring and development. Each student chooses the storytelling method he or she thinks will best serve his purpose. The choosing of a method is equally operative with professional story writers. But this choice and the ability to choose clearly implies a competence in the various possible disciplines. In so brief a treatment as I offer here, it seems wise to analyze just *one* good way to tell a story and to attain competence in that one discipline.

The well structured, true short story form examined here, which submits to the well defined discipline of the art form, has some specific characteristics unique to itself:

Definition of a short story: We should think of a

disciplined short story as a series of reported *scenes* in which a *causative situation* arises which requires a *deciding character* with a *governing characteristic* to try to solve some kind of *problem* along lines of action which he *decides* on as best for his purpose and which suffer *interruptions* or *intensifications* until he comes to the *result* of his final decisions. This condensed definition, with its key words, will be developed throughout the text of the book.

In a short story the reader is concerned with outcomes resulting from decisions made by the deciding character. The short story writer presumes that in the story all decisions and choices must be conditioned. In a story the central figure makes choices conditioned by his past experience which affects outcomes. He attempts to control his natural and human environment to his own desire. His decisions to solve his problem in certain ways pose for the reader the question: "Can the problem be solved under these conditions in this manner?" Answering this question, the writer generates a suspense very different from the interest found in narrative or essay and in the scenes to be found there. The posing of this question in a reported scene becomes the vital element of short story structure. Further, this sort of question invites the reader to participate in working out the solution in cooperation with the deciding character. What happens to him in the scene report happens also to us. Identification becomes more than mere sympathetic understanding. We, for a time, become the deciding character. This sort of identification is not possible nor necessary nor even desirable in a simple narrative, in which no crucial decisions are made and the characters accept what happens in a relatively passive fashion. In a short story such identification and participation are imperative.

If Laurel Ellison had written "So Young to Die," (which you should now read) reprinted in Part Two, as a simple narrative, the reader would be interested in it as an analysis of family relationships, and he would be delighted by the sensory but passive report of scene. He would find sympathy for Linnie and others in like difficulties. He would ponder the implications for himself and be reminded of his own experiences. He would be observant. But he would be relatively detached because the scene would not be directed and given vitality by a decision. Instead, as a short story reported in scenes, he is caught up into Linnie's experience. He does not merely understand her situation, the processes by which her personality is affected, the causes, the resolution. In a radically different way, he goes through the process himself, vicariously. Slowly, as the scenes unfold in the report, he, too, feels the need for acceptance. For the time it takes him to read the story and recover from it, he has so identified himself with Linnie as to become, with her, a little girl needing love. This sort of intense participation through identification is the special quality of the disciplined short story.

Scene the Basic Unit: All we have said so far has been by way of definition and will receive further development in later chapters. But in the beginning it is necessary to make clear the concept of scene as the basic structural unit of composition in a short story. You do not "tell a story"; you do not narrate a sequence of events. Instead, you conceive of the story as happening before you as on a stage (the actors, the settings, the speeches, the stage business, the lighting, and the sound); and you report what you see and hear and otherwise sense in the scenes. When the play requires a change of scene, you report the change. The process is dramatic, not narrative. But a short story is actually not a play. It happens in words, on a printed page. You transpose the stage setting to the imagined scene on paper and communicate with the reader in scene. How is this done? What constitutes a scene report? Let's examine the content of a sample scene.

What Is Scene?: Each of us exists actually in a scene. At any given moment, we operate within a specific context of time and place. Our sensory organs filter our experience of the world around us; we are subject both to the mood with which we initially approach the outside world, and the consequent effect that this world has upon us. The way in which we apprehend the world determines our personal point of view and the way in which we will act within that world.

Right now, as you read this, you are living a little scene, having an experience. How is this happening? What are the component parts of this experience? It is a certain *time,* say an autumn evening after dinner. You are sitting in a reasonably uncomfortable chair at a desk *in a room.* The *study light* is glaring down brightly on this page of print and throwing the rest of the room, if you will glance around you, into relative shadow. The drapes shut out the late evening light. You have a specific *purpose* in this scene: some fellow wrote a guide to short story writing and you intend to study it; you have certain subjective attitudes toward this purpose (the fellow, too, perhaps) which create a *mood* and which you could, if you wished, analyze. These attitudes as well as your physical position relative to the light and the book give you a certain way of seeing. For instance, if you get up and go over to that comfortable couch in the corner and lie down, the scene and your experience will change because the position has changed, though nothing else in the room moved. Test this assertion, if you will, now. So far you have isolated six identifiable elements of this scene that affect your experience: time, place, purpose, position, light, and character.

Now, continue this analysis of scene, extending it to include the functioning of your sensory faculties and their perception of the experience. You *see* this printed page and through it the images and symbols made on your mind by these words with their connotations and associations unique to you. During the glance around a moment ago you perceived all the details of *sight* that identify this place and this time: walls, ceiling, floor, chairs, table, desk, bed, all in minute detail of color and texture with their associations.

You can sniff and *smell* the study, with all the

private identifying odors, subtle, perhaps, but undeniably present and unique so as to make this room surely yours: fabric, textiles, leather, ink, typewriter ribbon and oil, lotion, your hands, that candy bar, and so on: all are part of the experience. If you were brought into this room blindfolded, could you identify it by the smell alone?

What are you *hearing?* Perhaps your breathing, and, since it is just after dinner, the inward sounds of the processes of peristalsis; if the room is quiet, the faint clicking from the kitchen of dishes being washed, the muffled monotone of the TV in another room, the faint movement of the breeze outside, a dog barking, unidentified sounds from the adjoining apartment, the quiet turning of these pages. All these consciously or unconsciously impinge on your hearing organism and become part of this scene experience.

What can you touch? Your clothing, of course, some of it tight and uncomfortable, the chair you sit in, this book with its weight and texture and flexibility. As you moved to the couch a moment ago, you touched other items. You feel the room temperature, and all these sensations you react to in some overt or subtle way.

Can you taste anything? Yes, your mouth and nasal membranes, perhaps your gum or the candy bar, the dessert you ate for dinner, or perhaps just your lipstick or your saliva.

What is being demonstrated here? Simply that you live in a scene uniquely and individually, that in fact we all do. No one else in the world can go through exactly the same actual experience that you have just analyzed. We do not smell alike, taste alike, see alike, touch alike, or hear alike. Each person is sensorily unique, since all experience comes to us through our individual sensory system. Further, we live constantly in scene, and we move from scene to scene. In the scene just analyzed we identified eleven elements: time, place, light, character, point of view, purpose, and the five senses.

Ideas for Study

1. Report precisely your own sensory perception of a room in your home. Try to report all eleven elements of scene.

2. Blindfold yourself and have a friend lead you into a familiar room. Stand still. Can you identify the room from its odor alone?

3. Stand for one minute in a room and list the sounds you hear, naming the source. Try not to use adjectives.

4. In what ways did the men in Apollo 11 use their sense faculties to explore the moon?

Actual and Imagined Scene: You will observe, in the following scene analyses, that the details are reported in consequential order; that is, one element rises from the preceding element and leads logically to the next; an event rises from the cause and moves toward the result.

This sequence of detail may be determined by the various purposes for the report. Perhaps the mood of the reporter decides the sequential order, as it does in "Blueberry Bread" and in "Uncle Josh." Or perhaps the physical relationship and position of character in the scene may determine the order of detail, as it does in "Age of Departure." Or perhaps the natural order of sense perception will conttol the sequence, as it does in Ernest Hemingway's "Big Two Hearted River" in the scene on the bridge or in the scene reporting Nick's preparation of his evening meal. Sometimes the physical progress of the reporter through a scene supplies the guide to sequence, as it does in this report of Paul's journey home from school in Conrad Aiken's "Silent Snow Secret Snow":

"On his walk homeward, which was timeless, it pleased him to see . . . the items of mere externality on his way. There were many kinds of bricks in the sidewalks, and laid in many kinds of pattern. The garden walls, too, were various, some of wooden palings, some of plaster, some of stone. Twigs of bushes leaned over the walls; the little hard green winter-buds of lilac, on gray stems, sheathed and fat; other branches very thin and fine and black and desiccated. Dirty sparrows huddled in the bushes, as dull in color as dead fruit left in leafless trees. A single starling creaked on a weather vane. In the gutter, beside a drain, was a scrap of torn and dirty newspaper, caught in a little delta of filth: the word ECZEMA appeared in large capitals, and below it was a letter from Mrs. Amelia D. Grayath, 2100 Pine Street, Fort Worth, Texas, to the effect that after being a sufferer for years she had been cured by Caley's ointment." As the boy moves onward his senses pick up added detail, and it is reported in the sequence of his progress.

In Sarah Orne Jewett's "The White Heron," Sylvia has climbed to the top of the tall tree and Jewett reports the expanse of scene thus: "Sylvia's face was like a pale star, if one had seen it from the ground, when the last thorny bough was past, and she stood trembling and tired but wholly triumphant, high in the tree-top. Yes, there was the sea with the dawning sun making a golden dazzle over it, and toward that glorious east flew two hawks with slow-moving pinions. How low they looked in the air from that height when before one had only seen them far up, and dark against the sky. Their gray feathers were as soft as moths; they seemed only a little way from the tree, and Sylvia felt as if she too could go flying away among the clouds. Westward, the woodlands and farms reached miles and miles into the distance; here and there were church steeples, and white villages; truly it was a vast and awesome world." Here the control over the sequence of detail is exerted by Jewett's need to communicate the effect of the height and distance and detachment and discovery, upon the little girl. The essential idea of consequence in this discussion is that you choose some control over the way you see the scene and let this control govern the con-sequential order of detail in your report.

Thus a scene has many functions in the story: To report sensory experience of time, place, and perception; to analyze and report character and purpose and motive; to fulfill the discipline of story structure; and to delight the reader with its clarity and sensitivity to artistic truth.

To conclude this chapter with another example, let's analyze one scene from James Aldridge's "Bush Boy, Poor Boy," reprinted in Part Three. Paragraphs six and seven will serve to illustrate the elements of scene in a story. We have been told in previous paragraphs of the story that "I" has determined to shoot a fox. In this scene, that is the purpose; "I," the character; Pental Island, the place; day, the time; day, the light; first person subjective, the point of view; and there are the senses of sight, soundlessness, smell, and touch. The mood is one of excitement. Here are all eleven elements except taste arranged in strict consequential order.

Ideas for Study

1. Concentrate on a small experience in your past and report it in a creative scene. Use eleven elements if you can, but do not invent. Be brief.

2. Think of a scene in a story you have read which remains vividly in your mind. Can you see it now? If possible, go back to the story and reread the scene. Identify the scene elements in it.

Some Useful Readings

1. Ghiselin, Brewster, ed., *The Creative Process, A Symposium.* University of California Press, Berkeley, 1952. Mentor, a division of New American Library, has a paperback edition of this book. You ought to own a copy. It is a series of thirty-eight statements on creativity by artists in many fields, including writing and, in my judgment, the best treatment of the subject in print. You should think of it as a basic text, and read it constantly. For a sampling of the book to our purpose read the

contributions by Mozart, D. H. Lawrence, William B. Yeats, Stephen Spender, Dorothy Canfield, Thomas Wolfe, Katherine Anne Porter, and Brewster Ghiselin.

2

Making The Scene Report

The Story Writer's Vocabulary: In the absence of stage props and actors, the writer must report the scenes of his story-drama with no tools except words. What can be said of the vocabulary he uses to transfer experience (character, event, place, lighting, mood, purpose, etc.) to the reader? We have long known that all our knowledge of ourselves and the world outside our skins comes to us through the five senses sometimes assisted by those scientific devices of tele- and microscopes, which extend sense perception in both directions. Awareness of this concept has been sharpened and deepened and extended of late by the electrifying events in space travel. If this is true, the writer who wishes to transmit the experience of the story character in a set of scenes must use words which work at the concrete sensory level of light, sight, touch, taste, and sound.

What sorts of words are most likely to be concrete? We would probably agree at once on nouns and words shaped from nouns. But not all these nouns evoke sensory experience. If you write "labor," you have not named a concrete sensory thing, but an abstraction. "Labor" might refer to the manufacturing of an electronic computer or to the making of a safety pin, to higher mathematics or ditch digging, with a whole range of economic and social implications. If you write "housing," you step down the ladder of abstraction to the building trades and what belongs to them and leave out all the rest. If you write "carpentry," all else is excluded; but you still cannot visualize it. Now, to make an enormous leap down the abstraction ladder: If you say "I saw John drive the 8-penny finishing nail into the door casing," you can point at it, photograph it, see it, hear it, feel it, and given the rest of the context, taste and smell it. The abstraction, "labor," has come to life in a concrete scene experience.

The short story writer can learn a great deal about the use of concrete terms from the work of a poet like Robert Frost. Here is another approach to "labor," from Frost's poem "Two Tramps in Mud Time." After reading this, can you visualize the scene? Do you need to ask whether or not Frost enjoyed his labor?

> Good blocks of oak it was I split,
> As large around as the chopping block;
> And every piece I squarely hit
> Fell splinterless as a cloven rock.
>
> You'd think I never had felt before
> The weight of an ax-head poised aloft.
> The grip on earth of outspread feet,
> The life of muscles rocking soft
> And smooth and moist in vernal heat.

Let's try again, with a different kind of abstraction. If my neighbor says, "Your flowers are beautiful," he leaves out all the sensory scene details which were present to make him offer the judgment. We are standing in bright, early morning sunlight before a bush of brilliantly full-blown American Beauty roses, admiring the color and the softness of texture and the rhythm and grace of the petal, inhaling the fragrance of the rose, aware of the morning coolness. His comment, which includes a subjective judgment, may be appropriate because the scene is before us; our shared experience needs no elaboration into words. But if he wrote the words in the absence of the things, the words would not transfer the experience. Being pure abstractions, they cannot report the sensory scene. We can point to the "roses" and photograph them. We can measure the temperature and test the texture. We cannot photograph "flowers" nor "beautiful."

We do not see a forest as a whole; we see a stand of lodge-pole pine. We cannot see a tree; we see a Lombardy poplar. And the farther down the ladder of abstraction we go to leaves and bark and light and shade and movement and so on, the more sharply do we receive a sense perception of scene. If in describing a leaf we use adjectives like "ugly" or "beautiful," we express a judgment related, not to the leaf, but to ourselves. If, instead, we say "green" or "serrated," we have presented sensory evidence, which can be transmitted to the reader. Good scene writing presents evidence rather than judgment. A story writer reports "things" as he senses them. To do this he uses concrete nouns and "naming" words shaped from those nouns.

Here is a fragment from the notebook of a visiting German student's story. "The first sunbeams slipped out of the cloud layer and gave the mist in the hollow a silver shining, when my brother, Havi, and I went through the high grass in our garden. The morning air was fresh, and every blade of grass gleamed of dewdrops shaped like pearls and glittering like crystal. We reached the wooden hut in which we have our garden equipment, and Havi went in. He came with a scythe, a wooden rake and a thin, grey whetstone. He pricked the stick of the scythe into the soft ground and rolled up his sleeves. 'Fine that you come with me, Sesi,' he said, and started to whet the scythe. The thin whetstone whisked along both sides of the scythe blade, and the tinny, whirring sound tickled my ears. I felt happy."

Can you sense the concrete quality of such verb forms as slipped, shining, shaped, glittering, gardening, pricked, whet (repeated three times), whisked, whirring, tickled? Can you sense the names implied in such adjectives as morning, silver, fresh, wooden (repeated twice), soft, and tinny? Thirty of the seventy words (excluding articles and connectives) are concrete terms. All of this passage is sensory report, except the last adjective. "Happy" is an abstraction drawn from the scene detail but not part of it. Coming at the end, "happy" seems to summarize the concrete words. It generalizes the mood and significance of the scene inductively, as abstractions properly do.

It will be apparent to you that the sharp sensory quality of exact concrete terms in this passage highlights by contrast the blurring of vision produced by clichés. When you read "dewdrops shaped *like pearls*" and "glittering *like crystal*," what happens to your visual perception? We can assume, I am sure, that Senti would not have chosen these stereotypes if she had been reporting the scene in her native German. As it reads now, we have the impression that, far from concentrating on scene to find the exact word which precisely reported the special look of the dewdrops in this morning air, she used the first English words that popped into her mind and thus weakened and dulled the report with the patent insincerity of a cliché. Using a cliché means giving up the search for the precise word. In effect it says to the reader: "You are not worth the effort it takes to find a fresh, exact word; I will use, instead a ready-made rubber stamp." The good writer, from the first declaring a war on the cliché, finds as his best weapon an intense concentration on the unique scene before him. As a secondary defense, some writers build slowly a list of words and phrases they know are liable to be clichés and then simply refuse to use them. One way or another all competent writers avoid the cliché.

Study this opening paragraph from Katherine Anne Porter's story, "Noon Wine":

"The two grubby small boys with tow-colored hair who were digging among the ragweed in the front yard sat back on their heels and said, 'Hello,' when the tall bony man with straw-colored hair turned in at their gate. He did not pause at the gate; it had swung back, conveniently half open, long ago, and was now sunk so firmly on its broken hinges no one thought of trying to close it. He did not even glance at the small boys, much less give them good-day. He just clumped down his big square dusty shoes one after the other steadily, like a man following a plow, as if he knew the place well and knew where he was going and what he would find there. Rounding the right hand corner of the house under the row of chinaberry trees, he walked up to the side porch where Mr. Thompson was pushing a big swing churn back and forth."

Miss Porter does not write "weeds"; but "ragweed"; not "trees," but "chinaberry trees"; and note the concrete verbs: "digging," "swung back," "sunk," "clumped," "rounding," and so on. In addition to the concrete quality of her words, the unobtrusive metaphor in such expressions as "tow-colored," and "straw-colored," merit your attention.

A prose comparison of two things emphasizes their points of similarity sometimes usefully in a report. A comparison is an expected thing; it discovers nothing we do not already know. Much more startling and revealing is the poetic metaphor, a device by which the reporter discovers an unexpected and surprising similarity in otherwise totally unlike things.

When a writer, working within the complex discipline of the story form and concentrating intently on making the scene report exact and accurate and capable of being transferred to the reader, comes to a detail of some experience which must be so exactly reported that it is not speakable in a prose statement, he often turns to metaphor for accuracy. Porter's choice of the words with their immediate evocation of the comparison of the boy's hair with scutched flax, and of the man's hair with straw, is the essence of the poetic act. In this passage the words focus attention on the exact color of the hair and, by implication, of its texture. How does a metaphor do this?

A good metaphor accurately reduces an abstraction to the concrete level of scene by observing that two things, literally quite different, are unexpectedly and startlingly and accurately alike in one special way. A metaphor is a poetic discovery. It has the parts of a triangle thus: A $\overset{C}{}$ B. In his scene the writer sees that, while A and B are in all other respects dissimilar, yet in one chosen detail, C, they are exactly alike. Miss Porter saw that, while the boy's hair was in all other respects similar to tow, yet in the exact *color and texture,* the hair was precisely like flax fiber after scutching. She saw that, in the precise shade *of yellow,* the man's hair and the otherwise dissimilar straw were exactly alike. Seeing the hair in these ways, we discover her report to be exact and accurate and evocative. You, as a prose writer, will use the poetic device of metaphor to reduce a difficult abstraction to the sensory, concrete terms of your scene report.

Careful selection of words for their connotative meanings will often be useful to you to make your scene report accurate and exact and to increase the depth of insight. The connotative meanings of a word go beyond its literal denotation, or definition, and rise out of association of the word with long established uses. These connotations inevitably cluster round the word and affect your use of the word in reporting exact shades of meaning. A good writer is constantly and acutely aware of the meanings he brings to his report by the connotative associations a reader is likely to attach to words.

For instance, if I write: "That man is a hog," I do not mean that he is literally a pig (which is the denotative meaning); I mean that he is a greedy, filthy glutton, because these connotative associations have grown up round our use of the word.

Think of the different meanings suggested by the two comments if I write of the President: "He has proved to be a great statesman" or "He has proved to be a great politician." Yet the acts and conditions referred to in each sentence may be identical; and the dictionary lists the denotation of these words as synonymous. The Random House Dictionary then offers this caution: "These terms differ particularly in their connotations: Politician is more often derogatory, and Statesman laudatory. Politician suggests the schemes and devices of one who engaged in politics for party or his own advantage. Statesman suggests . . . eminent ability, foresight, and unselfish devotion to the interests of his country. . . ."

Analyze the connotative power of the associations clustered round the word, "crumpled," in this line from

"Noon Wine" in the scene where Mr. Helton is punishing the boys. "Herbert's mouth *crumpled* as if he would cry, but he made no sound."

You will find pages 772-73 of John Ciardi's *How Does a Poem Mean?* a fascinating study of connotations. As a further study take any passage from a genuinely creative writer and test the propositions we have discussed here. In a given paragraph from any short story scene, count the concrete nouns against the adjectives. Test the adjectives and verb forms for their concrete derivations and connotations. Count the judgment adjectives. Observe the uses of abstract terms. Most of all, study how the words which seem exactly right to you rise directly from the scene context. I suggest you start this study with Hemingway's "Big Two Hearted River," Porter's "He," Conrad Aiken's "Silent Snow Secret Snow," or the stories reprinted in Part Three here.

Ideas for Study

1. Review the sections on nouns, adjectives, verbs, and verbals in a good grammar text.

2. Reduce the following abstract nouns to the lowest concrete level you can reach, stepping down the abstraction ladder as the text suggests: livestock, automotive industry, capitalism, love, protest, worship, marine life, bigotry.

3. Starting from each of the following concrete nouns, list words or phrases climbing the abstraction ladder as far into the abstract idea as you can go: a number 12 electric wire, a gasket in an automobile carburetor, a U.S. cent, a strip of bacon, a slice of bread.

4. Beginning with each of the following abstract ideas, descend the abstraction ladder as far into the concrete process as you can go: interior decorating, traveling by air, food processing, writing, merchandising. Concentrate particularly on using concrete verbs and verbals.

The Story Writer's Notebook:

". . . I remember exactly a balcony of a house facing a road, and, the other side of the road, pine trees, beyond which lay the sea. Every morning the sun sprang up, first of all above the horizon of the sea, then it climbed to the tops of the trees and shone on my window. And this memory connects with the sun that shines through my window in London now in spring and early summer. So that the memory is not exactly a memory. It is more like one prong upon which a whole calendar of similar experiences happening throughout the years, collect."
—Stephen Spender, *The Creative Process*

Beginning writers often ask, should I write from memory only, or can I *imagine* an effective scene or story? As the quotation by Stephen Spender suggests, the writing process is often too complex for such a clear distinction. In the work of writing, the imagined scene merges in the mind with the memory of actual experience. It shapes itself as scene or fragment of scene out of glimpses of the past which were vivid actually once, then were dropped into the reservoir of memory. Story writers all seem to have experienced these visualizations of scene out of memory. They agree that such visualizations cannot be willed into consciousness, but they rise unbidden during or after periods of concentration on the story scene. All this clearly suggests that the more experiences a writer can have, provided always that he is sensorily and fully aware of them and that they are natural, human experiences, the more material he will be able to store in memory and submit to the play of imagination as he works on his story scene. Imagination alone will not do; it must be grounded in actual experience out of memory. The trouble is, mainly, not that we do not have experience of story material, but that we are unaware of and untouched by that experience which is constantly around us.

What can you do to help develop this discipline of observation and memory and the mental trick of recall for use in the story scene? One good answer is to keep a writer's notebook. Nearly all fiction writers who discuss their art speak of their own notebook as indispensable. It is a very special sort of notebook, full of recorded sensory scenes. Make an effort to get down briefly, and with little development, the eleven components of a scene that has impressed you, exactly as you experienced it, with complete accuracy and candor. Try to get down your own unique sensory perception of it, and not to be influenced by the distractions of the expected or the established forms of other people's perceptions (another kind of cliché). Of this problem Hemingway said, in *Death in the Afternoon:* "The greatest difficulty, aside from knowing truly what you really felt rather than what you were supposed to feel, was to put down what really happened in action; what the actual things were which produced the emotion you experienced . . . The real thing, the sequence of emotion and fact which made the emotion and which would be as valid in a year or in ten years or, with luck and if you stated it purely enough, always . . ."

Here are some examples of what I mean by the scene subject matter of a writer's notebook, taken from student notebooks available to me:

1. The special fall of light and shadow on fallen leaves in a certain slant of autumn light.

2. The lift and fall of a sprinter's knees running the 220 in practice after school.

3. The feel of tall grass, dry in the autumn, against calf and ankle.

4. The smell of dry sage in a summer rain.

5. The sounds of a tugboat as it berths a freighter at a pier.

6. The psychedelic effect of faces on a crowded street as they come toward me in a steady flow.

7. The smell and shadowy shapes of a deserted stage after a play.

8. The strange illusion of moving forward while watching a stream flowing under a bridge.

9. The change in perspective on seeing a familiar street from the top of a skycraper.

10. The look on the face of a disillusioned child.

11. The sight of a dead sparrow in the frost-hardened rut of a dirt road.

12. A familiar room, bare after the movers have left.

All these fragments of scene reports were later developed, and still later fashioned into finished products and printed in the school literary magazine. They had been tucked away much earlier into a writer's notebook and forgotten, until involuntarily they fused into creative imagination during a period of intense concentration on report of scene in a story.

Sometimes the notebook contains full development into sentence and paragraph. More often the notes simply show lists of words or phrases recording the sensory content of a scene. But they all help to capture the experience and lodge it in memory to be recalled at the right time and place.

In addition to the record of sensory scene, other elements of short story structure belong in the notebook, sometimes independently of scene. Interesting ideas centering about a problem faced by someone, how he solves it or doesn't, his motive, what prevents solution, what finally results—these ideas may not appear in the notebook as scene; but they may later become part of scene in a disciplined story.

A writer also collects striking characters, people known or unknown to him who attract his attention by virtue of some intriguing or interesting gesture or movement, or physical aspect, or idea expressed and so on. These may be reported in the notebook, briefly or in detail, but always in a concrete sensory vocabulary. What people say, how they say it, the exact word and locution, the gesture, facial expression, movement, tone, and volume, all may usefully be recorded, even though disconnected at either end.

As a story writer you are always looking for material. You know you will eventually scene your story about a character facing a problem that he wishes to solve. Thus, causative situations which require decisions interest you. They become apparent around you in real life, in newspapers, in TV.

For example, the following three newspaper excerpts

taken at random report situations which might give rise to problems and suggest solutions:

1. Plain City, January 27: "An eleven-month-old baby girl is reported happy and healthy here after a brush with death. Little Donnell Butler, daughter of Mr. and Mrs. Grant Butler, of 3377 Pioneer Road, was rushed to the McKay Hospital after she choked on candy. Mrs. Butler said that her baby started choking on candy apparently given her by an older brother. The baby had started turning blue . . ." This story would obviously center around the brother and his family relationship, the tensions, his problem, and the dangerous act. It is a situation with most of the story elements present or strongly suggested. The question the brother asks is: "How to get attention, when the baby apparently absorbs all my mother's love."

2. New York, (AP), January 27: "Authorities say a father of four, who was arrested on drug charges, used teams of children to peddle narcotics. District Attorney David Epstein said: 'This man conducts a Fagin-like activity in the sale of drugs . . .' " Here, the situation is extreme and foreign to most persons' experience, but by making one of the children the protagonist, the writer can supply concrete human motivations from memory. Some of the questions suggested were: how to escape the father's domination; how to establish personal self-respect; how to escape arrest; how to "succeed," even when success means peddling drugs.

3. Local press, January 27: "Some 800 Union Pacific Railroad workers walked off their jobs at midnight in Ogden, leaving the rail industry at a standstill in the wake of a nationwide strike." What problems will be faced by the young employee and his family under this stress? What solutions will he find?

These clippings obviously offer ideas for story material. They stimulate invention. They may usefully go into a writer's notebook. If the note can be recorded in the form of a scene or partial scene, so much the better.

It will be apparent from all this that you, as a story writer, work at it all the time. You develop a writer's penchant for sharp observation and awareness, and for storing potential material—sometimes on the spot, more often from immediate memory—in a writer's reservoir, the notebook. I strongly suggest you keep the sort of notebook we have been discussing. It will help you develop: awareness of the world around you; skill in sensory observation, skill in making scene; and a sharper response to experience, and therefore more insight into the meaning of experience.

Ideas for Study

1. With a good friend taste some unfamiliar food. Compare the notebook entries of your taste report. Do the same for touch: stroking a cat, holding an ice cube in your hand, going barefoot.

2. Listen to a record or tape playing one of your favorite pieces of music. Make a list of all the words you can think of to report the sound. Do any of them exactly report your own private perception of the sound? Find one or two of your own words that do fit your private hearing exactly. Put them in your notebook. How would you report the sound of a tuning fork, or traffic, or running water?

3. Study your newspaper and list as many potential story situations as you find. They needn't be spectacular. List some characters with problems.

Some Useful Readings

1. Ciardi, John and Miller Williams, *How Does a Poem Mean?* 2nd Edition. Houghton Mifflin, Boston, 1975. Pages 779 to 795, though directed at poetry, are especially enlightening in a study of the vocabulary of creative writing in the short story. Ciardi treats fully the meaning produced by connotation, association, and emotional response to words.

2. Langer, Suzanne K., *Philosophy in a New Key: A Study in the Symbolism of Reason, Rite and Art.* 3rd Edition. Harvard University Press. This is a profound but readable study of creativity as manifested in various arts. You should study the entire book, but

the first five short chapters deal especially with man's symbol-making propensity. They will help you to understand the creative process with words.

3

Some Scenes Analyzed

Before leaving the preliminary comments on scene as the basis of short story structure, we ought to be even more specific by analyzing some full scenes. The first four scene reports, written by students, originally appeared very sketchily in their notebooks. Then they were developed into full scenes and later used, sometimes much altered, in a full length story.

The comments accompanying each scene report seem to me the best part of this book. I urge you to adopt the following procedure throughout these analyses: first read the text of the scene through, without reading the parallel comments; then, read again each section of the scene and the accompanying comment parallel to it. This means at least two readings of the scene, once for the content and once again for the analysis. Though this procedure makes for slow and painstaking study, your attention to detail here will reflect itself in your own writing.

Scene Analysis:

BLUEBERRY BREAD
by Olivia Bertagnolli

TEXT	COMMENT
1. On Saturday morning, Clara walked to Leo Auff-	1. Time, Saturday morning; place, top step of the

man's house on the corner and sat on the top step of the porch where the sunlight pooled and dropped into the narrow slats between the steps. The sun warmed the wind, catching in the leaves of the winter-twisted oak that pushed away from the side of the house.

2. The light wedged between the bars of the porch rail, creeping along the edge of the porch until it reached the legs of Leo Auffman's wicker chair. Clara loved Leo Auffman almost as much as she loved Mrs. Auffman, with her fat, squat body and her powdered wrinkles that squeezed

3. out around her neck in rolls, and her blue eyes that lost themselves in chasms of wrinkles when she laughed.

4. No one in the world could make blueberry bread the way Mrs. Auffman could. When the sun had pushed the shadow of the oak tree on to Leo Auffman's shed, Mrs. Auffman brought Clara yellow flaked milk in a heavy enameled cup and blueberry bread wrapped in a red checkered tea cloth.

porch of Leo Auffman's house on the corner of the same block; lighted by the sun—pooling, dropping, warming, catching, wedging, creeping, and reaching (notice these concrete verbs and verbals); six sight details. Note the con-sequence of wind and leaf movement.

2. Light is repeated, and it precedes sight con-sequentially; characters, Clara and Leo. Olivia establishes the point of view; it is through Clara's consciousness that we sense the scene and, therefore, it is Clara with whom we identify ourselves. She gives Clara an identifying characteristic of affection for the Auffmans. We do not (con-sequentially) see Mrs. Auffman till Clara remembers her.

3. She reports Mrs. Auffman, a third character, with detail of sight.

4. Mrs. Auffman now functions as breadmaker and hostess; light repeated; sight continued, and place, all developed with fifteen concrete details.

5. Filmed bubbles thickened into heavy yellow foam, nibbling against the whiteness of the cup. The larger bubbles burst into rich froth, clinging to the sides of the cup when Clara lifted it to her lips.

6. The cool film glistened on her lips and pooled under her tongue, seeping into her throat; and it was whipping cream, and chunks of smooth yellow cheese hidden in the bottom of her lunch pail; curled cheese on apple pie and white-milk cheese dipped in bee's wax hanging in the fruit cellar. Clara's tongue pushed softly against the roof of her mouth, milk oozing into her throat when she swallowed.

7. Mrs. Auffman unfolded the warm towel with her short fingers. Steam peeled over the curled edges of the basket, and the smell of blueberries spilled over Clara, carrying on the wind. Mrs. Auffman clutched the basket in her brown hands and held the cloth back with her fingers. Clara lifted a firm yellow square from the top. Butter glazed her fingers, and steam dropped from the bottom crust into her hand. She held the crust to her lips, and the steam singed her nose and lips. Fat, yellow squares of sweet bread stuffed with plump

5. Notice the use of concrete verbs and verbals again, to report the senses: sight (movement, color, texture); touch (temperature and texture); and taste. Note also the orderly sequence of detail.

6. Now Olivia reports the senses further in an exploration of both actual impressions and the associations which the impressions evoke: whipping cream, chunks of cheese, apple pie, bee's wax, fruit cellar. Note the use of texture in the last sentence. Clara's character is developed by the choice of detail—these choices would occur only to Clara.

7. Mrs. Auffman reported further; she moves in her appointed purpose to serve the bread. A report of the smell and a qualifying repetition of the wind. From the first paragraph the report of smell moves into a delightful report of taste intensified by touch within the mouth, and temperature and texture and sound in the ears. Sight is reported fully. Thus even so short a sketch is a full scene: light, time, place, character, purpose, point of view, and the five senses—all eleven elements. Notice the metaphoric quality of such words as "fat,"

blueberries, so bloated with thick purple juice that they popped inside her mouth when she bit into the crust; the wrinkled skins burst, pushing out the hot breath and ebony meat of blueberries. Golden crusts against buttered bread and lips: Bread, alive with blots of blue mold spreading through moist curds of air; salted breath, juice-drenched crumbs rolling over her tongue, crunching inside her ears, clinging to her teeth until the sweet frothy milk carried them away.

"bloated," "wrinkled," "golden," "blots," "blue mold." This sort of poetic compression, most useful in short story reporting, occurs throughout the scene. It is accomplished mainly with nouns or verbs or verbals. Olivia uses adjectives sparingly and usually with concrete connotations: narrow, wicker, blue, heavy, yellow, rich, cool, smooth, short, brown, fat, yellow, sweet, plump, thick purple, ebony, golden, olive, moist. She avoids adjectives which make judgments. She doesn't, for example, say the bread is delicious.

In addition to observing Olivia's sensory perception, you can learn a good deal from her about the uses of verb forms. Underline all the verbs and verbals in her sketch. Examine them to find what senses they report and how they move the scene forward. You will notice that Olivia has avoided the careless use of "to be" forms. These become necessary only when the function of the verb is to link or to establish identity or to state an abstraction. They can almost never report scene. She has also avoided the weakness and circumlocution produced by passive verbs.

Note carefully how much detail of Mrs. Auffman's character Olivia develops through the sensory report of scene, of which the character is an element. What do you know, and feel, now, about Mrs. Auffman?

Ask yourself the central questions: "Can I experience the scene she reports? Did the blueberry bread happen, also, to me? To the degree that you can answer "yes," the sketch succeeds in transferring experience.

Ideas for Study

1. Write several sentences using passive verbs. Then rewrite the same content with active verbs. Note the change in emphasis and meaning.

2. Write a report of an actual scene in which eating is the central focus.

Scene Analysis:

Penny Allred's notebook supplied the following scene, later made into a story. In this sketch John is her brother, and the time is the day before he leaves for military service. How does Penny use the concrete details of their hike to convey to you her emotions about his departure?

From AGE OF DEPARTURE
by Penny Allred

TEXT	COMMENT
1. He was up ahead of me on the trail, standing in the bright sunlight; and I could see the sweat darkening his hair along the back of his neck.	*1. In a short paragraph Penny reports character, and some characteristics; place; light; sight; and implications of touch in temperature and moisture.*
2. "Wait a minute," I said, and I sat down on a rock at the side of the trail. "I've got to empty my shoes."	*2. Positioning of characters in place; point of view represented by "I."*
3. John came back making little rock slides with every step. When he got to the rock he stopped and bent down to roll up the cuffs of his Levis. His crew cut was so short and thick on top	*3. Sound here. Notice how the order of the items in the report is governed in consequence by the action; all is in exact time and place sequence. For example, "I" cannot report the crew cut,*

you could hardly stand not to reach out and pat it with the palm of your hand. I almost did, but I decided not to. I knew it would feel like the soft brushes they use on new babies' hair.

4. When he looked up it seemed almost as if I'd never seen him before, as if I hadn't looked at him really. As if I'd never seen his eyes squinting against the sun and making little wrinkles at the corners just tighter than laugh wrinkles, or ever seen his brows drawn together in half a scowl like that, or his teeth white against the tannedness.

5. He picked up a rock, his body moved back with his arm, his white shirt stretched tight, and the rock went up—a black fleck in the blueness. In a second it came crashing down through the oak brush leaves at the bottom of the trail.

6. After that everything was quiet, and the only things moving were the red ants and sometimes a quick, sand-colored lizard.

7. Sometimes I think, "I dreamed I was doing this. Everything looked and smelled just the way it does now, and everything hap-

with its revealing implications of touch, until John bends over. What is the effect of Penny's metaphor in the last sentence?

4. Notice how the objective details of sight evoke and explicate the subjective feelings and give the reader an insight into the character of both John and "I." Here is light repeated effectively, to produce facial expression, and then light again in the contrast of face and teeth. Note carefully the effect of this repetition and the technique of variation in repetition.

5. Movement, and sound and contrasting absence of sound come together, with some parallel microscopic sight detail and light.

7. Smell comes in now, and an interesting subjective reaction in recapitulation which reveals the character of "I." All elements of

pened this way." That's how it was then. I knew I had seen John throw a rock just like that, and after the crashing down in the leaves, felt the heat and quietness. I hadn't dreamed it though. It really had happened just like that.

scene except taste are present in this brief report.

Ideas for Study

1. List Penny's active verbs and note their concrete quality; count the uses of "to be" verbs.

2. Go for a climb, or merely walk around the block, and report in a scene a one-minute pause. Include at least ten elements of scene in your report.

Scene Analysis:

The next passage presents a two-scene report which was a notebook entry at first and became a short story later. The full story reports dramatically the experience of a little girl as she watches her uncle decapitate a rooster for the family dinner. In her eyes, the event takes on the surrealistic quality of a nightmare. Notice how from the beginning, Janet selected words connoting more than the simple description of gruesome details: "bloody," "egg yolk," "smeared," "moldy," "spilled," for example, in the first paragraph.

From UNCLE JOSH
by Janet Hurst

TEXT	COMMENT
1. A bloody, egg-yolk sun dropped on the top of the sandhill, smeared itself over moldy clouds, and spilled purple ocean tide along the edge of the sky.	*1. Scene One: light at first and, by implication, in the details of color, time (sundown); note here the connotative force of the words and their effect on mood;*

The little girl leaned against the back door, her body overcast with the shade of the house, and shadows deepened in the folds of her dress.

She looked after Uncle Josh as he scuffed through the leaves, that crackled like dry onion skins, toward the coal shed, his bib overalls hanging loosely from his stiff shoulders. She followed him then, slowly, her hands behind her.

2. Uncle Josh's shadow slithered under and over the autumn leaves in front of him, and his right leg dragged along the ground, tugging at the grass and leaving a clear trail through the leaves. His shadow pounced on the coal shed door and loomed up above him one and a half times his own length.

3. The little girl shuffled behind him and stared up at him through heavy eyelashes; the door creaked as he yanked it open, turned, and looked down at her. The vein that stood out on his forehead like a purple cord caught some shadows from the sky and rode with them to the two lines that deep-

character, with approximate age; Janet gives the point of view to the little girl; we do not see into her consciousness, but we see the scene through her eyes; light persists and changes; place; purpose—to observe and stay close to Josh; sound clear and sharp; sight detail; we not only see Uncle Josh but begin to understand the emotions he causes in the little girl.

What does the report of the girl's hands reveal about character?

2. Scene Two: a change of place (to the coal shed). Note how the report carefully includes the transition from place (the back door) to place (the coal shed). Light is reiterated and altered. Josh is given a character tag of lameness and deformity; his shadow becomes another sinister being, more than human-sized. Notice "slithered" and "pounced," and "loomed."

3. Another glimpse of the girl, sound again, sight; note how Josh comes alive and is revealed both in aspect and in character in the dialog. Why "crunched"? Careful consequence of action here, sharp sight report. The mood of gloom and foreboding is heightened by vocabulary. Notice also the

ened above the bridge of his nose. "Better get in the house, girl," he said, and he crunched over coal, reached up for the ax that hung on the wall, and took it down.

metaphoric report of Josh's facial expression. The point of view does not vary.

4. The blade of the ax glinted in the little girl's eyes, and she shook her head slowly, sideways. Still staring at the blade, she backed out into the leaves; but when the door of the coal shed started to close, she reached out quickly and stopped it.

Dust, silver in a streak of light from a crack in the roof, reached out and pulled the little girl into the shed. The door creaked shut, and she stood there, covered with half darkness.

4. Again the play of light and shadow and careful consequence of detail in the report. Note how effective is a judicious repetition of scene elements, especially light. Why does Janet say that the lighted dust pulled the girl into the shed?

Ideas for Study

1. What is the mood or tone of this report; and how is it produced?
2. Visit a butcher's shop, meat market, barnyard, or meat-processing plant and observe the preparation of meat for eating or sale. Report this in a scene. Count the elements.

Scene Analysis:

It may be well now to examine the expert use of scene by professional writers. The first example is from Richard Wright's symbolic short story, "The Man Who Lived Underground" from the collection Eight Men. *In this scene, the man has just let himself down through a manhole into the sewers.*

From EIGHT MEN
by Richard Wright

TEXT	COMMENT

1. The cover clanged into place, muffling the sights and sounds of the upper world. Knee-deep in the pulsing current, he breathed with aching chest, filling his lungs with the hot stench of yeasty rot.

From the perforations of the manhole cover, delicate

1. Sharp report of sound, announcing place (underground), sight, touch (temperature), smell, point of view, all in two sentences. Note the concrete verbs and verbals: clanged, muffling, pulsing (a metaphor), breathed, aching, filling. Wright evokes smell with both noun and adjective.

2. lances of hazy violet sifted down and wove a mottled pattern upon the surface of the streaking current. His lips parted as a car swept past along the wet pavement overhead, its heavy rumble soon dying out, like the hum of a plane speeding through a dense cloud.

2. Now light, consequently, as the eyes accommodate it in the darkness, reported in metaphor (lances). Report of sound, associated with the character's gesture. Note the concrete metaphoric verbs: "sifted," "streaking," "swept," "dying."

3. The odor of rot had become so general that he no longer smelled it. He got his cigarettes, but discovered that his matches were wet. He searched and found a dry folder in the pocket of his shirt and managed to strike one; it flared weirdly in the wet gloom, glowing greenishly, turning red, orange, then

3. Odor again and its effect. The character's action follows in strict consequence. Now a detailed report of light, including minute particulars of color and effect. Note that the order of light detail is carefully reported as it would be seen in the given situation—no more, no less. Trace throughout the other details Wright uses to establish the character's physical presence within the scene.

4. yellow. He lit a crumpled cigarette; then by the flickering light of the match, he looked for support so he would not have to keep his muscles flexed against the pouring water. His pupils narrowed and he saw to either side of him two steaming walls that rose and curved inward some six feet above his head to form a dripping mouse-colored dome. The bottom of the sewer was a sloping V-trough. To the left, the sewer vanished in ashen fog. To the right was a steep down-curve into which water plunged.

4. *Read the passage omitting all adjectives. Is there anything lost? Examine the connotations of such words as "steaming," "mouse-colored," and "ashen." Analyze the effect of the vivid verbs and verbals: "flickering," "pouring," "dripping," "vanished," "plunged." In spite of the nightmarish scene it reports, this vivid passage seems unostentatious, even restrained, because Wright uses words with such precision. The sensory accuracy of the report makes it realistic and believable as well as emotionally powerful.*

Ideas for Study

1. The uses of light here deserve special attention. In what specific ways does the report of light affect the scene? Answer the same for smell.

2. Visit some dark, strange place and strike a match. Report the scene. How does the darkness accentuate other senses besides sight?

Scene Analysis:

Here is a scene from a very different writer and from a very different sort of story, set in an English moor landscape.

From FELIX TINGLER
by A.E. Coppard

TEXT

1. . . . Hungry at last and tired, he sat down and

COMMENT

1. *Character,   insight (hungry and tired), place,*

leaned against a large ant hill close beside the thick and perfumed furze.

and point of view are established, with details of touch and smell. Time has been reported in a previous paragraph.

2. Here he ate his cake and then lolled, a little drowsy, looking at the few clouds in the sky and listening to the birds.

2. Now come sight, hearing, and light. Taste is implied. A little of "his" character shows in "lolled" and "drowsy."

3. A flock of rooks was moving in straggling flight towards him, a wide flat changing skein, like a curtain of crape. One of the rooks flapped just over him, it had a small round hole right through the feathers of one wing. What was that for?

3. Note this sequence of "zooming in" from the broad to the close, microscopic view. How is metaphor used to evoke the sight of movement? Study the concrete verbs here. Note the indirect report of the character's thoughts. What weight does it provide?

4. Felix was just falling asleep, it was so soft and comfortable there, when a tiny noise, very tiny but sharp and mysterious, went "Ping!" just by his ear, and something stung him lightly in the neck.

4. Detailed report of sound, then touch, made sharper by contrast with the character's sleepiness and sense of comfort. The name of the character appears.

5. He knelt up, a little startled, but he peered steadily under the furze. "Ping!" went something again and stung him in the ball of his eye. It made him blink. He drew back; after staring silently at the furze he said very softly, "Come out!" Nothing came; he beckoned with his forefinger and called aloud with friendliness, "Come on, come out!"

5. Sense report is repeated from a more minute point of view; sound here in the direct dialog, touch, and character insight. Note the phrases accompanying dialog, and the strict consequence of action and observation, as the character moves closer to the source of the "ping."

6. At that moment his nose was almost touching a brown dry sheath of the furze bloom, and right before his eyes the dried flower burst with the faint noise of "Ping!" And he felt the shower of tiny black seeds shooting against his cheek. At once he comprehended the charming mystery of the furze's dispersal of its seeds, and he submitted himself to the fairy-like bombardment with great glee . . .

6. Gesture, sight, and touch, now in extreme close-up and detail. Coppard concludes the scene with insight into character and setting, broadening the meaning, giving direction and purpose to the scene. In this scene, all eleven elements appear. Did some things happen to you as you read it?

Ideas for Study

1. How does the detail of the hole in the wing feathers focus attention on the flight? How does Coppard achieve elsewhere the "close-up," microscopic point of view?

2. Some readers might see this passage as a "description of nature" only. What does the scene reveal about Felix's character, and how?

3. Try reporting several scenes from the following list. These reports will be of actual experience, no fiction here at this time. You may cover a very brief time or a limited area, but make the reports as sensorily complete as you can. Use the eleven elements of scene as a checklist against which to measure your report: light, time, place, purpose, character, point of view, smell, hearing, taste, sight, touch. Then submit your report to the class audience, to a friend, or to the editor of your school journal to test it for creative communication. Will they be able from your words to share your experience? Keep these scene reports in a notebook you have set aside for this purpose.

SUGGESTED SUBJECTS FOR SCENE REPORTS:
Drinking a glass of water from a tap.
One minute of traffic at a busy intersection with an

officer directing, or a minute of freeway traffic as seen from an overpass.

A police arrest.

The view from a high building.

A supermarket fresh-fruit or vegetable counter.

The first minute after you enter your living room, arriving home.

A hospital corridor.

Your mother's or father's face or hands.

A heavy machine in action.

A laborer at his work.

The lobby of a large hotel (or small hotel).

One block in a slum section of town.

A running stream.

One minute of dialog. (You may use a tape recorder if you like, but be sure to report the accompanying gestures and expressions and tone.)

Some Useful Readings

1. Hayakawa, Samuel I., *Language in Thought and Action,* 3rd Edition. Harcourt, New York, 1972. Here is an excellent treatment of the objective report. It pays specific attention to the uses of abstract and concrete vocabulary, to tone, to slant, and to the operation of language in a practical world.

4

Dramatic Character Reporting

General Order of Scenes: We have talked about scenes in such detail because they form the basic units of the story. But they do not, of themselves, make a story; and ordinarily one scene has not sufficient space to make a story. Some questions have arisen: How do you arrange the scenes so as to make a well-disciplined short story? What goes into scene besides sensory report to make it a sequential dramatization of events? What controls the order of scenes? What creates suspense? And so on. The next four chapters will furnish some answers. It is useful at this point to remember that a short story is a series of reported scenes, in which a causative situation arises requiring a deciding character with a governing characteristic to try to solve some kind of problem along lines of action which he decides upon as best for his purpose and which suffer interruptions or intensifications until he comes to the end result of his final decisions. The definition supplies its own clues as to the content and sequence of scenes.

A story is made up of three separate and distinct parts. You can make a picture of a story as a series of three stage settings, one or more for each of the three parts of the story, thus:

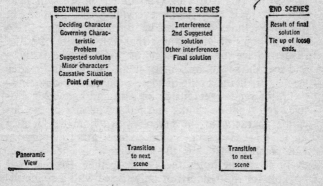

BEGINNING SCENES	MIDDLE SCENES	END SCENES
Deciding Character Governing Characteristic Problem Suggested solution Minor characters Causative Situation Point of view	Interference 2nd Suggested solution Other interferences Final solution	Result of final solution Tie up of loose ends.
Panoramic View	Transition to next scene	Transition to next scene

Of course, these three essential parts may be expanded into as many scenes as are necessary to report the story. But the content of the three story parts, though it may be rearranged within the part, remains as the diagram indicates.

The vocabulary of structure used here will receive full treatment as we proceed through these chapters, but at this point you should see that a writer thinks of a story as being built of three separate parts. Each part accomplishes specific necessary functions in the story, as indicated in the diagram. He keeps the content and purpose of each part separate from those of the other parts. All the story parts occur within a general panoramic view, and transitionary sentences link the parts and the scenes making up each part. Further, the writer thinks of a story as a drama, acted out on stages (scenes) in sequence. We will examine the structure of the story part by part and elaborate the vocabulary of the definition as we use the words.

Deciding Character: According to the implications in our definition of a short story, the deciding character is the individual who is affected by or who tries to decide issues facing him in the solution of his problem and to choose, rationally or subconsciously, or impulsively, a solution. He is the person with whom the reader identifies. He may not be the most important character or the most interesting personality (though he usually is); but unless the point of view (about which we will hear more later) is omniscient, everything that happens in the story comes to the reader through his senses. He takes a point of view which makes it possible for the reader to see into all aspects of the story: he is there and sees the scene, or someone tells him and the reader listens, or, if the point of view is subjective or omniscient, the reader gets inside his skin and knows his motives and what he thinks and feels. This use of the deciding character as the person with whom we identify ourselves provides unity and concentration of purpose and perspective. Thus the deciding character reports every scene; he holds the story together. He makes it possible for the reader not only to see with a single vision but to identify himself emotionally and intellectually with the character. When this is accomplished successfully, the story is completely believable and capable of being experienced because everything that takes place in it takes place in and for the reader, too, as reported in Part Two. "I" is the deciding character in "Grandpa" and in "Feels Like Spring." Linnie is the deciding character in "So Young to Die."

To illustrate further, from the stories printed in Part Three, the deciding character in "Bush Boy, Poor Boy" is "I"; in "Through the Tunnel" it is Jerry; in "Sled" it is Joey; in "Wullie" it is Billie ("I" is a narrator); and in "How Mr. Hogan Robbed a Bank" it is Mr. Hogan.

Ideas for Study

1. Identify the deciding character in some stories familiar to you.
2. List five problems you have actually faced to which you had to decide on a solution. Did your first solution work? Did you decide on a second solution?

The Governing Characteristic: In a piece of writing so brief and so concentrated as a short story, the kind of extended development of changes in character which we associate with the treatment in a novel is usually impossible. Ordinarily, there will be time only for a clear presentation of one governing characteristic. This characteristic may be altered by event, or affected by it, but will remain essentially static. Yet the actions and decisions of the deciding character, to be believable, must correspond to what a reader knows of his total personality. To achieve this reality in a story, the author gives the deciding character a governing characteristic which determines the direction of his choices and decisions. In an early scene, (usually the first scene), he faces his problem, which, though it must be clear to the reader, may not yet be clear to him; the reader watches him *choose* what he *considers* the best *solution* to it and begin *acting on* that decision. The report of this decision demonstrates his governing characteristic in action.

In "Feels Like Spring," Milton Kaplan has the deciding character think: "I'm all alone in New York City, and I guess I'm kind of shy and don't make friends easily." As explicitly as that he states the governing characteristic which controls all of "I's" choices and actions. And just as explicitly he has "I" choose action, as when he thinks: ". . . she'd say quickly, 'Oh, I beg your pardon,' and I'd lift my hat politely and answer, 'That's perfectly all right' and I'd smile . . ."

Another good example of this technique is the dialog in the first fourteen paragraphs of "Sled," Part III, in which the problem, the governing characteristic, and the decision are all sharply apparent during the exchange, not necessarily to the boy, who acts largely on impulse, but to the writer and the reader of the passage.

To keep the governing characteristic always before us, most writers choose some appropriate phrase or word, a gesture perhaps, which will remind us of the governing characteristic. They repeat this character phrase often in well-chosen places. Thus a full paragraph of scene report of character can easily be later re-evoked by a brief, remembered key phrase. Writers usually use such phrases to keep before the reader what structural elements are basic to the story: governing characteristic, scene, and physical appearance, etc. These phrases will be pointed out more fully in the specific comments. But we need here to have the concept of repeated phrases used for repeated evocation.

How is the deciding character presented in a short story? Remember that the basic unit of structure in reporting a short story is the scene, with its eleven elements. One of these elements is character. Reporting character is as simple in concept as this: if your scene includes character, and your report of scene is accurate and complete and to the point, and your visualizations are clear, then of necessity your characters will emerge clearly and pointedly and visually, and the reader will have insight into and empathy for that character. You will have little or no static "description" of character relatively independent of the story structure. The character will act in a scene, will display in the scene by his action and speech and thought, his governing characteristics functioning in the scene as it is reported. He will be identified by a physical characteristic, face, gait, tone, size, age, etc., which clearly identifies him and which is repeated often enough to become familiar. You do not "develop character" in a short story in the sense of reporting complex changes in it as you would do in an essay or novel. You report a character as he occurs in scene, and as the events there affect him.

This is not to say that character is less important to your story than scene or structure. Rather it demonstrates that the way to the handling of a deciding character and his governing characteristic is through faithful scene report. A story moves forward with directness and intensity and all deliberate speed from the first sentence. You do not delay the story for a static description of a character, independent of scene. Rather, a character evolves from the scene of which it is a part.

The scenes in "Bush Boy, Poor Boy," Part III, report two characters, Edgar ("I") and Roy. How does Aldridge evolve these characters from the scene report? In the first five paragraphs he presents the panoramic view. In the first paragraph he tells us that "I" is a boy, poor, living in the "bush," and we know his driving ambition. In the second we learn he is motherless, is no scholar, envies Tom, finds teachers and policemen unfriendly, is a joke to the town boys, is an expert in the "bush" life and a failure in town, and how he envies Tom. In the third paragraph we learn he supports himself by hunting, and we assume his age at between ten and twelve. In paragraph 4 we see again his stubborn determination and discover the physical tag that he goes to school barefoot. With no static description in four paragraphs of the panoramic view, we have a working notion of Edgar, including his age, sex, size, dress, poverty, and his governing characteristics of determination and envy, including his relationship to his peers— all necessary to a clear understanding of the elaboration of character to come in following scenes.

In paragraph 13 we learn that Edgar has problems expressing himself before adults. The next tells us more about the facets of character we have already seen. The governing characteristic has been demonstrated in a minor action. And in paragraph 15 the minor actor, Roy, has been introduced with his tag of age, repeated three times in four sentences. In paragraph 38 we have Edgar's exact age, a necessary bit of information, always most useful in understanding a character. Paragraphs 57 to 70 and paragraph 77 demonstrate in scene action both Edgar's stubborn streak and his kind of shrewdness, both part of his governing characteristic, and also his failure to realize his true psychological situation.

The first fourteen short paragraphs of "Through the Tunnel," Part III, present the two characters. Though the mother seems very minor, she functions to make the situation seem realistic and to elicit from Jerry some revealing comments. We learn of the deciding character, Jerry, his name, age, swimming experience, and his strong but unformed desire for independence from his mother inhibited by his native courtesy to and affection for her. In paragraph 16 we see the desire for independence linked to a "craving that filled his whole body." Thus his governing characteristic comes to light in the report of scene. Paragraph 17 rounds out the character. The governing characteristic is repeatedly tagged in all succeeding scenes. Reference to his mother's white arms gives, by suggestion, the tag of whiteness with all its many connotations to Jerry.

Notice the revelation of age and self-image in paragraph 19: "They were big boys—men to Jerry" and in "He felt . . . proud of himself." And do not miss the insight provided in paragraphs 24 and 30. These help us understand not only Jerry but all boys who have tasted failure.

Study how Lessing uses dialogue to reveal Jerry's intense emotion and preoccupation in one word; "Yes," in paragraph 53.

Notice what a sharp flash of insight into character can be produced in one line: "which now seemed a place for small children," in paragraph 57.

We have seen character revelation and elaboration in scene and dialog. In paragraph 60, first sentence, we see the reporter intrude his own comments on character, breaking the point of view. Which of these techniques seems more effective to you?

Notice how all of this detail of characterization is brought into play at the moment of Jerry's final decision, paragraph 62, second and third sentences. The governing characteristic operates at all decisive moments of the story.

In "Sled," Part III, Joey's governing characteristic is his willingness to deceive. He avoids the outright lie, but acts surreptitiously and deceptively. How are these characteristics elaborated? Notice carefully how the scene is reported. The dialogue of Scene One, paragraphs 1 to 29, shows clearly that his apology is a fraud, his obedience enforced and resentful, his antipathy for his sister deep but controlled for selfish reasons. He is impatient (the buttons). He respects the authority of his mother only superficially and for selfish reasons.

Again in the second scene, paragraphs 36 to 39 show clearly his propensity to deception, together with a kind of arrogance which is inhibited only by fear of authority. All this character elaboration is reported in the dialog and accompanying phrases of scene.

In paragraphs 45 and 46 we are reminded that Joey is only a little boy, with whom we can sympathize in time of stress, but his governing characteristic does not change.

In paragraph 56 of Scene Eight the spoken question, which is really a major decision, though it may have come impulsively with no deliberate attempt to injure, displays sharply Joey's governing characteristic of deceit. The inarticulateness of Joey in the dialogue in paragraphs 61 to 71 further elaborates this. And Joey's lack of reasoned intent does not blur this decision for us.

Even after the events of Scene Eight, which present every opportunity for Joey to have changed his character, he remains essentially true to his governing characteristic in the last two paragraphs of the story. Note that in these paragraphs occurs the only development of character outside of dialogue.

Ideas for Study

1. Invent a short scene which clearly demonstrates some facet of a speaker's character.
2. Invent a short scene in which a character's action demonstrates something about his character.

3. Select a scene from a short story familiar to you in which action demonstrates character.

4. Select a scene in which a decision is made which clearly demonstrates the functioning of a governing characteristic.

5. Select a scene in which a physical tag is repeated effectively.

Minor Characters: As a general rule, if you can report the story with one minor actor, don't use two; if you can do it with two, don't use three. Minor characters must have a necessary part to play in the story structure. According to the part they play, they possess a distinguishing characteristic and a physical tag. This part may be merely to round out a scene and give reality to it, as do the parents in "Wullie," Part III. A minor actor may serve to give insight into and to elucidate the deciding character by dialogue or action, as does the mother in "Through the Tunnel" and as do the mother and sister in "Sled." Or he may function fully in one of the structural elements, as, in "Bush Boy, Poor Boy," Tom Woodley produces the causative situation, and Roy takes part in the interferences and accompanying decisions. He may add reality and humor, as do the townspeople in "How Mr. Hogan Robbed a Bank," Part III. The point is that minor characters never appear in a short story unless they serve a specific, necessary structural or reportorial (scene) function; and their appearance in the story is limited to the performance of that service. When you plan your story, use what minor characters you need, but introduce them into the scene sequence only on specific purpose.

The Problem: Think of the concept of Problem flexibly. The problem in a short story is whatever causes decisions by the deciding character, whether reasoned or involuntary. The problem may involve physical endurance: how to perform the feat of holding one's breath long enough to swim underwater through the tunnel. Or it may be how to develop sufficient skill to catch a twenty-pound cod and shoot a fox. Or the problem may be psychological, as in "Sled": how and whether to deceive. It may be largely an intellectual idea or theme or an investigation into ethics or morality or religion, as in Katherine Anne Porter's "He," Sherwood Anderson's "Unlighted Lamps" and in "Wullie." Or it may be very simply how to rob a bank, or how to get a grandfather to let you ride a horse, as in "Granpa," or how to meet a girl and alleviate loneliness as in "Feels Like Spring." Even in such a lengthy and involved masterpiece of psychology and physical endurance as Stephen Crane's "The Open Boat," the problem is simply how to survive a shipwreck.

The point about Problem is that, though it may be complex and involved or simple and apparent, it must be capable of suggested solution. The deciding character must be able to try to find ways to solve it, to carry out the suggested effort. The decision to act may be simply on impulse without reason, or it may be involuntary or even unconscious or felt blindly. We do not always know clearly why we act, and the deciding character may not know. He may be unaware of his motive. But to the reader and to the writer the decision to act on a suggested solution must be clear. On this point of choice and decision and its effect hang all the elements of suspense in a short story. We ask the question: can the deciding character, given his governing characteristic and the conditions of the problem, solve it along the lines of action he has been impelled to follow? The conditions giving rise to this question have all been clearly reported in the scenes of the *Beginning* of your story. And if the story has been slanted to a theme or idea, this has also been reported in scene. We have mentioned theme earlier. Perhaps a word or two concerning theme or idea may be useful here.

The Story Idea. Most good stories develop either subtly or ostensibly an intellectual idea. It may, in fact, be the writer's reason for writing the story in the first place. But preoccupation with the theme must never override or cloud the reporter's purpose: to record a series of dramatic scenes. The story is never a tract; it is always a play.

To be specific, in "Granpa" the old man says:

"You've found out that there are things in life that people think they want, but when they get 'em, they discover they didn't want 'em at all." All the events of the story support this thesis, but it does not appear anywhere in the story independently of structure. If it did, we would have a tract.

The theme in "Wullie" is not stated as succinctly as it is in "Granpa"; yet it is presented in the scene report throughout. For example: in Billy's reaction to the gun, paragraphs 4 to 15, 32 to 36, 68 to 73, and on thus to the dramatic finale. The theme of everyone's individual responsibility to ensure the humane treatment of animals, is developed fully by scene report, with no outside-of-scene essay on the idea, or even a statement of it.

Once we have made identification with the character, we follow with suspense and participation his blind or rational attempts to solve his problem if he can. And though later interferences (*Middle*) may impede the solution and perhaps require a change in the suggested solution, the problem and the character remain structurally the same and intact throughout the *Middle* and the *End*.

Ideas for Study

1. Select an actual problem which you are facing now. This is for real.

2. Make a full statement of it as it exists.

3. Invent a deciding character, giving him specific limitations.

4. Restate the same essential problem as it might be faced by this imagined character.

5

More of the Beginning

Panoramic View: As each scene exists in its own time and place, so, in the series of scenes called a short story, the scenes exist in a larger time and place. You begin the story by establishing, early in the series, (usually in the first scene), this general setting, called the panoramic view. In this view you provide the general setting in which the succeeding scenes take place. This panoramic view performs the same function as does the TV camera, when it shows first an entire general panorama, then zooms in closer to the immediate subject and shows a sequence of detailed scenes. The panorama will include at least time in general and place in general, and sometimes light, character, and purpose, and some of the senses. Do not ignore it. How and whether you use it will, of course, depend on you and your material and your intent. The panoramic view provides a framework necessary to a clear understanding and perception of entire sequence of scenes.

To illustrate the report of panorama, look at the story "Bush Boy, Poor Boy," in Part Three. The panorama begins with paragraph 2. This is not scene, but narrative. We are given the country (Australia), the province and town (Victoria and St. Helen), which you can locate on any good map of Australia, the river (Murray), the distance up the river from town (three or four miles), and the fact of the Bush, where the story occurs, all of which, if we wish, we can look up for clarity. The time is the era of the Model T. Some of the deciding characters' characteristics and limitations are reported. All the scenes of the ensuing story take on reality and visual clarity from our knowledge of the general panorama in which they occur.

To illustrate further, in Doris Lessing's "Through the Tunnel," the panoramic view is reported in paragraphs 1 to 4. Much less detailed than that in the Aldridge story, the report supplies only the minimum necessary panorama: the place is a foreign seacoast on a resort beach, with a wild, rocky bay juxtaposed to a crowded, sandy beach; the time is summer, and the English boy and his mother are vacationing. To locate the scenes following, this is all we need to know. A panoramic view should supply only the general setting necessary to a comprehension of the succeeding scenes. Preferably, you report it as part of the opening scene, or you may narrate it, if the scene seems ill advised.

Causative Situation: As often as possible, a story ought to, and usually does, open at the causative situation. This is the point at which his problem becomes clear to us and impelling to the deciding character, and demands of him that he try consciously or subconsciously to find a solution to it. It is, of course, apparent to you that you, as a character, are at this moment facing actual problems, some of them perfectly clear to you, others blurred or merely felt vaguely, many of which will eventually arrive at a time when you will be forced to make a decision about solving them: school, family, social life, job, career, neighborhood —all offer problems. Many of them, luckily, need not be solved at all, since they will solve themselves; many can be held off indefinitely. These are not yet ready to become short story material. But a situation may arise for some of these problems which will make a decision imperative; for example, an acceptance into two schools at the same time. Either would present you with a causative situation, requiring decision, and they suddenly turn a merely interesting problem into short story material. In actual life, as in a story, the situation may come on us unaware and not clear, but in a story it must be clear to the reader.

To illustrate the causative situation in action, study

the references to scenes in these stories from Part Three:

In "Bush Boy, Poor Boy" paragraph 2, the final sentence, the arrival of Tom Woodley and his success with the cod and the fox is causative. It requires a decision from "I." In the story "Wullie," paragraph 1, the birthday with the gift of the .22 rifle is causative. It sets off the series of decisions leading to the final result. In the story, "Sled," paragraphs 1 to 3, the snow, coupled with the mother's demand for a humiliating apology, is causative. Perhaps nothing in the sequence would have happened without the snow and the humiliation being juxtaposed at exactly this time. Though the impulse to revenge may not be conscious to Joey, it is clear to us.

The scenes ought to move progressively forward from the first situation. Writers try to avoid the necessity of a flashback scene or a narrative passage. But it is probably better to flash back than to begin too early, before the problem presents itself as causative. Beginning too early before the causative situation arises requires a slow, static process through exposition to the first decision. This, too, is objectionable. Flashbacks are used only to bring in absolutely necessary information, which given earlier would have delayed too long the introduction of the causative situation.

A flashback may be reported in a remembered scene, as it is in Scene Two of "So Young to Die," where Linnie remembers Mart's illness. Or a character may relate the flashback scene. It may otherwise be reported in non-dramatic narrative. While it always impedes the forward movement of the story, it is sometimes preferable to a delayed start.

Point of View: So far we have seen six essential, structural elements which should be reported in the Beginning of the story. One more crucial element of structure must have been established before we can end the Beginning, and begin the Middle with the first interruption. No disciplined short story is possible unless the reader can identify with the deciding character, who attempts to control his own destiny, exercise choice, make determinations. So that for the time it

takes to read the story and recover from it, the reader
becomes, psychologically, the deciding character; and
the problem becomes his own.

To achieve this intense participation by the reader,
short story structure requires the adoption of and faithful adherence to a point of view which will permit reader identification with the deciding character. He is the
actor in the scene through whose consciousness all events
of the action, all sensory perception, all decisions, and
all results come to the reader. Through this character's eyes, ears, nose, fingertips, the reader *experiences*
the story, not merely understands it. This discipline of
identification requires that the writer understand the
points of view that are available to him, that he choose
the one best suited to his purpose, and that he not for
an instant shift from that point of view.

The point of view of "So Young to Die" is the one
which, for many good reasons, is the most commonly
used in short stories. Linnie is the deciding character.
All of the story comes to us through her consciousness.
It is through her sensory system that we perceive all
the scene detail. And, in addition, we use her voice and
think her thoughts and share her feelings. Further, we
are not aware of anything in the story that she is not
aware of. We do not know, for instance, what her sisters or her parents are thinking or doing except by their
direct statement or by inference from Linnie's report.
We do not know what is going on in a room until
Linnie enters it and reports. This point of view is often
called, appropriately, the *third person subjective.* Should
it be violated for a moment, if, for example, we had
observed a scene between the parents and the sisters,
before Linnie entered, our hypnotic identification with
Linnie would have been interrupted and the tension ir-
reparably lessened. Such a violation of point of view
would, like the snap of the hypnotist's fingers, bring us
rudely back from Linnie's world of the forlorn little girl
into our own world of adult security, and spoil the
story.

"Sled," "Through the Tunnel," and "How Mr. Hogan Robbed a Bank" are all reported in the third person

subjective point of view. The advantages of this point of view for a full report of inside-and-outside-the-skin analysis of the deciding character and his story are many and obvious. It permits the reporter to remain noncommittal; it allows full exploration of idea, theme, and especially of motive; it offers a variety of means by which the events and scenes of the story can be reported to the reader; it thus encourages that most precious of short story qualities: a complete reader identification with the deciding character; it permits untrammeled and faithful report of dialog; and the third person subjective does all this with much less difficulty for the writer than does any other point of view. For these reasons, most writers adopt it.

The *third person objective* point of view also permits the use of a deciding character. Though it cannot report what is going on inside the character's skin, it has the advantage of being at once completely believable, because the reporter's perception of the external world is limited, like the reader's, and like our real life experience, to actuality, to what the reporter can sense objectively. Since such a report cannot examine the subjective thoughts and feelings of the deciding character, it must supply convincing outward evidence of inward events. The reader, therefore, is probably slightly less than ready to make full identification with the feelings of the deciding character. He cannot participate fully in the decisions, and he cannot be so sure of motive. With story material that requires analysis of motive, of feeling, of subjective reaction, as in the story of psychological insight like Aiken's "Silent Snow Secret Snow," the objective point of view is often inconveniently restrictive. In "So Young to Die," Linnie obviously required subjective analysis, and Laurel wisely chose the third person subjective as the appropriate point of view.

In "Wullie" the point of view is given to a narrator, "I," who, while Adams reports him subjectively, himself narrates Billy in third person objective as we actually see people in real life. We are never told anything about Billy which "I" cannot sense objectively. We induce his feelings, motives, thoughts, solely from the evidence supplied in "I's" objective report. And part of the interest in this point of view is like the game we play when we actually try to penetrate to the mind and spirit of a real person. This little excerpt from Roger Martin DuGard's novel *The Thibaults* illustrates the power of objective reporting to reveal insight without going inside the skin of the deciding character:

> The first thing Antoine noticed was the lamp which a woman in a pink dressing gown was lifting with both hands; her ruddy hair, her throat and forehead were flooded with the lamplight. Then he observed the bed on which the light fell, and the shadowy forms bending above it. Dregs of the sunset, filtering through the window, merged in the halo of the lamp, and the room was bathed in a half-light where all things took on the semblance of a dream. Antoine helped M. Chasle to a chair and approached the bed. A young man wearing pince-nez, with his hat still on, was bending forward and slitting up with with a pair of scissors the bloodstained garments of the little girl. Her face, ringed with matted hair, lay buried in the bolster. An old woman on her knees was helping the doctor.
>
> "Is she alive?" Antoine asked.
>
> The doctor turned, looked at him, and hesitated; then mopped his forehead.
>
> "Yes." His tone lacked assurance.

Besides the objectivity of the point of view here, it is worth noting the scene detail and the careful process of con-sequence in the reporting. We get insight into Antoine by following the scene through his eyes. What, for instance, is told us by the "mopped his forehead" gesture about the nature of Antoine? Student writers usually find the third person objective point of view a more difficult discipline to manage than any other; but it is fun to try, and it gives reality and belief to the reader when it is successful. It offers severe, but not impossible, impediments to identification.

Stories in the *first person subjective* point of view often tend to be somewhat self-conscious, and often, in the hands of a beginning writer, sound too much like a "true confession." Further, the results very often seem improbable and the story lacking in credibility. If the scenes report events which involve the physical safety of the deciding character, it is difficult to ask convincingly: "Can he survive along the lines he has laid down?", when it is already obvious that he has survived to tell the story. Identification, for these reasons, is sometimes difficult, and the reader sometimes finds himself reluctant to participate, as in Mr. Poe's stories of horror. In most of these we are persuaded that the events ought to be horrible, but we refuse to be horrified. Yet in "Granpa" and "Feels Like Spring" the first person subjective seems completely appropriate and useful, and identification seems complete and unembarrassed. This is true because the events and reactions of these stories are subject matter a person might be expected to talk about. They read a little like reminiscences.

The *omniscient author*'s point of view is seldom used in the short story, but is usually reserved for the novel. In this point of view the writer sees all and knows all and enters into all characters and events. There is no single character who, like an X ray, furnishes the reader with eyes and ears. Thus no identification with a single character is possible, and no participation follows. Yet a few very successful stories have used this point of view, one of the best being the justly famous "The Open Boat" by Stephen Crane. However, even in this story, moving and beautifully disciplined as it is, the complete entrapment into experience, the hypnosis, the intense participation through identification, fails. We are fascinated, engaged, sympathetic, moved, but we do not identify. We do not experience the story, rather we observe it happening.

The main points made in this section on point of view are these: First, that the problem of securing reader identification with the deciding character involves a wise choice of point of view, and thus a knowledge of the choices available. You choose the point of view best suited to your purpose. Second, having decided on your point of view, you do not change it even for a sentence or a word, but keep it clear and undeviating to the end. Third, most writers find the third person subjective point of view most useful to their purposes. You must evolve your own best way for each story you write.

Before moving into Chapter Six, we ought to sum up the first five chapters to see how far we have come in the structure of the story: We have reported the panoramic view in which all the scenes of the story will occur; we have noted the causative situation, which precipitates the decisions and solutions; the deciding character, with his physical tags and his governing characteristic has been established, and a point of view has been chosen and identified for him; minor actors with their appropriate characteristics and functions have been introduced; the problem has been clearly defined; the deciding character has made his first decision as to a suggested solution to his problem. We are nearly ready now to consider the structure of the Middle of the short story.

But throughout all this discussion so far, one vital element of short story reporting has been largely absent; that is the use and discipline of dialogue. It is now time we considered it.

The Uses of Dialogue: When two characters come together in a scene they will talk, *unless you have explained their silence.* But in so concentrated a series of scenes as you are writing and as this discipline requires, dialogue must have purpose. A writer uses dialogue to develop insight into character or motive, to report sensory scene without using static description, and to develop the story's structure, that is, the governing characteristic, the decision, the solution, and so on. You will discover that in most good short stories, just as in actuality, a character exposes his personality by his choice and use of words, his idiom, his tone, his face, and his gestures. The situation and the structure must inevitably determine for the writer what words to put into his character's mouth. To illustrate these uses, read paragraphs 25 to 42 of "Bush Boy, Poor Boy," excellent dialogue.

A writer trains his ear to identify the various sounds

of actual dialogue around him. How do people actually carry on a conversation? Exactly what is the idiom peculiar to dialogue? How does the vocabulary of dialogue differ from that of straight narrative? When is the use of dialogue indicated or appropriate? Training yourself so that you can report the dialogue in a scene accurately and with validity requires a good ear, willingness to listen attentively and self-consciously; and it takes practice. Put scenes involving dialogue into your notebook. People all around you are talking. Pay attention to the sounds, throat noises, dialect, idiom, pitch, volume, words, and gestures. All this usually goes too fast for recording, but you can get a good deal of it down in your notebook from memory. The tape recorder is helpful, if you can use it unobtrusively, because you can play it back and study it. Try to catch what people say and do in such situations as on a first meeting, in a serious confrontation, while giving reasons or answers, in anger, in joy, and so on.

But you must be aware that the dialogue you will write into your story will not be actual dialogue, and your story characters will speak, while always in the manner and idiom people use, still they will speak under your conditions and to your purpose, and never at random as in actuality. So you must carefully study the dialogue of fiction, not only the speech, but gestures, movements, facial expressions, tones of voice, which become a part of the speech in accompanying phrases, all helping to effect insight into character, motive, structure and scene.

Accompanying Phrases: Very often in dialogue, the accompanying phrases, which consist of everything that is not part of the actual conversation, can convey as much as the speech itself. Through his description of what goes on inside and around his characters, the author reveals to us both the nature of his characters, and his own overall purpose in the story. In analyzing dialogue, note particularly the placement of the "he said" (or "she said"), or identifying clause. Where does it occur in the speech? How often is it repeated? When does the verb vary from "said" and what are those variations? As an exercise, read the following sentences, and keeping these points in mind, decide which of the passage works best:

1. "This is something you must decide for yourself. I cannot help you. Maybe you need legal advice," she said, thoughtfully.
2. "This is something you must decide for yourself," she said, rearranging the papers thoughtfully. "I can't help you." She looked at him intently. "Maybe you need legal advice."

You can easily demonstrate the uses of accompanying phrases in dialogue by leaving them out of a passage, then juxtaposing the original version and noting the difference in effectiveness. For example, read the speech lines alone in this conversation from Steinbeck's "The Red Pony," where Gitano comes to the farm gate. Without the accompanying phrases, the conversation goes like this (italics mine):

"Do you live here?" *the old man said.*
"Yes," *said Jody.*
"I have come back," *the old man said.* "I am Gitano, and I have come back."
"It's an old man," *he said to his mother.* "It's an old *paisano* man, and he said he's come back."
"What' the matter now?" *she asked.*

The speech lines are recorded here, just as Steinbeck supplied the words. But note what happens to the dialogue when we quote it in full, with the accompanying phrases (italics mine). Analyze them to see what, besides an identification of the speaker, they contribute to character insight and to structure. For example, what scene elements do they add? How do they illuminate character? What part of the story structure (check list) are they contributing? Note carefully the position and nature of the "he said" clause:

The old man drew close to the gate and swung down his sack when he confronted Jody. His lips

*fluttered a little, and a soft impersonal voice came
from between them.*

"Do you live here?"

*Jody was embarrassed. He turned and looked at the
house . . . and toward the barn . . .* "Yes," *he said,
when no help came from either direction.*

"I have come back," *the old man said.* "I am
Gitano, and I have come back."

*Jody could not take all this responsibility. He ran
into the house for help, and the screen door banged
after him. His mother was in the kitchen poking out
the clogged holes of a colander with a hairpin . . .*

"It's an old man," *Jody cried, excitedly.* "It's an
old *paisano* man, and he said he's come back."

*His mother put down the colander and stuck the
hairpin behind the sink board.* "What's the matter
now," *she asked patiently.*

What can be learned of Jody from the phrase, "and
the screen door banged after him?". Or what of the
Old Man from "fluttered a little" and "soft impersonal
voice"? And how is the mother illuminated by the
colander gesture and by the word, "patiently"? The
best way to learn about the uses of dialogue in fiction is
to study it in good writers.

Examples of Dialogue: In "Wullie" the two characters are contrasted expertly in the dialogue from paragraphs three to six; "I," concerned with the gun and
shooting, Billy, with the beauty of the snow. This passage defines the governing characteristics of each boy.
Again note the contrast and the sharpened report of
structure in the ten paragraphs from 13 to 23, especially in paragraphs 15 and 16. Watch the position
of "he said" as near the beginning of the sentence as
possible, and observe the report of movement and scene
in the accompanying phrases. The details of structure
move clearly into play in the dialogue in paragraphs 44
to 61. In this passage the two characters are clearly
exposed; the decision to cure Wullie is plotted; there is
sharp insight into motive. An interesting fact is that
the phrases and the content of what is said, rather than
any distinctive difference in the vocabulary or tone of
the boys' speech, develop the character differences.

In "Through the Tunnel," Doris Lessing limits the dialogue to only ten short paragraphs, mainly at the conclusion of the story. She does this because Jerry and the boys did not understand each other's language and because the sequence of events permitted her to report scenes in which Jerry is alone. Although some stories use no dialogue at all, for instance, Kafka's classic "The Burrow," or Jack London's "To Build a Fire," most stories use dialogue much as we have described it.

This brief discussion of dialogue should make clear several points: First, dialogue, if used at all, should always develop some aspect of structure or scene. Second, the vocabulary, tone, idiom, should be accurate for the situation, the character, and the scene. Third, the accompanying phrases offer the key to the dramatic report of dialogue. And four, the "he said," or identifying clause should be placed at or as near as possible to the beginning of the speech and restrained usually to simple declarative verbs.

What makes writing good is the writer, his revelation of self in his story. The scenes of the story visualized in imagination out of memory as only the individual writer sees them, with detail drawn from the well of sources that come from his own experiences and from reading and thought—this will make his story creative and valuable. His ability to concentrate on scene so that characters come clear, insight is vivid and revealing, action is con-sequential and purposeful—this ability gives point to the short story discipline.

Ideas for Study

1. Report a specific use of the "zoom-in" technique on TV you have observed and describe how it assisted you in the process of viewing subsequent detail.

2. List some actual problems you have faced and invent situations which might precipitate them into short story material.

3. Write as accurately as you can, a short actual exchange of dialogue, reporting all accompanying gestures, facial expressions, vocal tone, body movement.

6

The Middle of the Short Story

Interferences: The Middle of the story presents
scenes in which the solution decided upon by the deciding character in the Beginning scenes suffers an interference of some kind which forces the character to re-
evaluate the situation and to make a new decision for a
more effective solution. An interference may be the result of opposing forces, or it may be, but rarely is, an
accident. The solutions, however, must always come out
of the kind of character you have reported. The decisions may rise from impulse, or blind unawareness, or
by deliberate choice of the deciding character, but never
from accident.

Accidents are common enough in real life. In actuality they sometimes account for vital decisions and
much knowledge and character development. But a
story is not life. It is an artistically disciplined representation of life. It has its own limitations, one of these
being the necessity of insuring identification by the reader with the deciding character and participation with
him in his efforts to solve his problems. This need requires that the deciding character exercise choices, that
he try to control his own destiny. But accidents are, by
definition, out of control. You do not *decide* to have one,
unless it be by suicide. Hence, the only place for accident
to function in a story is as an interference to the solution. Here accident becomes a part of the story structure and is legitimate and sometimes useful. It is well
to caution against too much use of accident even in
this part of structure, however, because it is liable to
irritate the reader by appearing more like author
meddling than true interference. In any case, if you

use an accident, it ought to be explained, as, in "Wullie," Rafe's ability to hit a dog with one throw of the bottle. The suspense of the story lies in the reader's uncertainty about whether the solutions decided upon will eventually solve the problem. And a writer can keep on reporting interferences as long as he thinks he can maintain the suspense and increase the tension. In the Middle you should take care to report the scene detail in strict con-sequential order to insure continuity within the scene and between scenes.

Sometimes the interfering element does not change the suggested solution but merely intensifies the situation and makes more immediate and more pressing the need to solve the problem. Or it may clarify the problem both to the reader and to the deciding character. Whether the Middle scenes report interference or intensification or both, the suspense increases with each interruption, and the reader's concern over the central question heightens. There is a sharp rise in the intensity of the reader's participation and a clarification of his role as partner in the solving of the problem. When the writer reports the final interference or intensification, he has come to the end of the Middle of his structure.

There is little opportunity in the Middle for developing complex changes in character. The writer more adequately sharpens and delineates, and defines and elaborates the governing characteristic, but he seldom radically alters it. He makes sure that the tag of the governing characteristic appears with increasing clarity at all moments of decision. He repeats the physical tag of his character's appearance at all structural points and wherever a clear visual image of the character seems necessary. Where sensory report is indicated to assist in the complete experience of the structure or the character or the idea, he carefully performs the report of sensory scene. He faithfully limits narrative to those transitions between scenes which are necessary for clarity and con-sequence.

Some Examples of Middle: In "Bush Boy, Poor Boy" the problem facing "I" is how to make clear his superiority over Tom Woodley. The first solution is to shoot a fox and catch a codfish. The middle begins at the first interference, the accident of seeing the fox without a gun, reported from paragraphs 6 to 12, with effects continuing much longer. The solution is now altered to include only catching the cod, paragraph 14. The second, major, interference is reported in the scene of the tangled lines and Roy's error, beginning paragraph 105 and on to paragraph 116. The final solution comes in the scenes reported between paragraphs 138 and 148, and at that point the Middle ends. Up to this point we have seen no change in "I's" character, but looking back after the end, we can identify the influences which brought about this change.

In "Through the Tunnel" Jerry's first solution is to join the native boys and promote a friendship, though he cannot speak their language. The Middle begins as this simple solution fails when they "proceeded to forget him" in paragraph 17. The next solution Jerry decides on is to entertain them with clowning, in paragraph 23. This solution fails in miserable embarrassment. His third solution is to find the tunnel in paragraph 31. This solution fails because he is not properly equipped. His fourth solution is to obtain the goggles and try again. From this point on the suggested solution remains the same (to go through the tunnel), and the difficulties are intensified not by a change in solution but by the sensory report of scene to the end of the Middle, which comes clearly with success at paragraph 79. This story will bear careful study as an excellent example of both interference and of intensification and of a sharp increase in intensity brought about by the structure and by faithful report of scene in the Middle.

You will notice that in "Wullie" the minor actor, Rafe, very usefully supplies most of the interruptions and interferences. In "Through the Tunnel" the mother, a minor actor, supplies intensification. In "Bush Boy, Poor Boy" Roy interferes, assists in the solution, and instigates decisions. Thus it is clear that minor actors take sometimes a prominent part in the Middle story structure. As with the deciding character, the minor actor's physical tags are repeated for visual clarity at all points where they function in the structure: Rafe's vicious temper, Roy's age, Mother's delicacy and white skin, and so on. When it is clear to the reader that the deciding character has made his final decision as to the best solution to his problem, you have reached the end of the Middle of the story structure. Some comments on the End will come next.

Ideas for Study

1. Choose one of the problems with its causative situation which you listed in the exercise at the conclusion of Chapter Four. Invent a solution. Invent an interference which is not accidental. Report all this.

7

The End of a Short Story

The End Prepared For: The End section of a story reports the result of the deciding character's final decision on how to solve the problem, which may include a change in the character of the deciding actor. This result, whatever it turns out to be, physical, intellectual, emotional, ought to be and usually, but not always, is inevitable. That is, the reader should have been prepared for it from the first scenes. He ought to be able to say of the result: "Yes, that's right; given the structural components of the story and the decisions made, and the scenes as reported, it could have ended only thus." This requirement of inevitability must be kept in mind during the reports of all decisions, all solutions, all interferences, in each part of the story. The result reported in the End has thus been carefully and progressively prepared for. This does not mean that the end should necessarily be foreseen. Many stories depend on the element of shock or surprise to make the End effective, "Wullie," for instance. But looking back on the story, after the end, the reader should be able to see its inevitability. The End of "Wullie" is inevitable, and we accept it. In "Sled" and "Bush Boy, Poor Boy" an alteration in the character of each boy has been prepared for, and is, in fact, the point of each story.

The writer has one more obligation in the End part, and that is to make sure that all loose ends of scene or structure or character or event have been so neatly tied up that he can say of any unfinished business, as Kipling so often did, "but that's another story." The reader should be satisfied that the present story has come to its appointed end.

Some Endings Examined: In "How Mr. Hogan Robbed a Bank" the End begins with paragraph 26 and ends only twenty-four short paragraphs later. Beginning with paragraph 26, the result of all of Mr. Hogan's decisions unfolds rapidly and is completely reported by the end of paragraph 29. The remaining paragraphs neatly tie up all loose ends.

In "Sled" the End begins with paragraph 61. Everything after that, including Joey's change of attitude in paragraphs 95 to the last, results from the last decision. It is fair to say that this change was intended as perhaps the theme of the story. But it seems not inevitable and is not really necessary to the story. If it is retained because it is the point of the story, then Mr. Adams ought to have been more careful in preparing us for it in the scenes of the Beginning and especially those of the Middle.

In "Bush Boy, Poor Boy" the End begins with paragraph 158. Whatever happens after that will be the result of "I's" final choice. He lets the fox get away when he might have killed it. But this act is now consistent with all we have learned about "I." It has become clear to us during the slow elucidation of his character in the Middle scenes that, while neither his governing characteristic nor the problem has changed, the boy's realization of himself and his situation was slowly dawning into the insight reported in the End result.

If you wish to incorporate character development into your story, you would do well to study how Aldridge reports crucial scenes in terms of increased awareness by the boy of himself and his aspirations. This is a story of no change in aim or intent of structure, but change in self-realization, in awareness, in comprehension of his place in the scheme of things. If the boy had been carrying his rifle on his first encounter with the fox, he certainly would have killed it. The events reported after that: his nightmare, Roy's influence, the fishing episode, the story of Roy's misfortune, and so on, are all reported so sensitively that we observe the changes in the boy (even though we are unaware of their significance); and we are not surprised by the End. Instead, looking back on the story, we are likely to say, "Ah, so this is what it was all about." This is good short story discipline.

Ideas for Study

1. Write an End for the story you projected in the exercises for Chapters Four and Six.

8

The Application of the Discipline

Getting Started: It may be convenient, now, to reduce items we have covered in the foregoing discussion of short story discipline to a compressed, summarizing checklist for planning and revising your short story. The list asks questions on the main problems of structure in an order closely following that of our chapters.

Some writers outline each scene in advance of writing, showing in the plan of scenes each of the structural elements to be reported in each scene, and something of the sensory content of each. Their outline follows the pattern of Beginning, Middle, End, and accounts for structural detail in each part. The actual writing can then proceed with a minimum of organizational difficulty. This is a good, methodical way to get a story started and down on paper while the general ideas are fresh. And it keeps the total story in mind for a long time, with little danger of losing detail and direction during the involved process of writing. Such a checklist as the one offered here will assist in this kind of planning.

Other writers have the general idea and the continuity of the story well in mind. They write detailed scenes in which certain already-foreseen events take place, completing them as units more or less independently of each other and not necessarily in continuity. Then with the individual scenes largely finished, they rearrange and order the scenes into continuity, taking out and putting in as the need rises and the story develops. The checklist assists in such a reordering and in the revision of scene report. Still other writers seem unable to visualize the story as a whole generally or to foresee specific events, or even to know the end in advance. They may have a character in mind which they wish to structure into a deciding character. Or perhaps they have a delightful passage of dialogue that can be worked into a scene. Or a sensory scene opens up before them which they must capture. Or they are taken by an intellectual idea, or a mood or feeling or theme, which they can exploit in a scene. To wait until all this takes shape in the mind as an ordered story would postpone writing indefinitely. In any case, the story begins with writing, and this writer begins by reporting scenes more or less helter-skelter until the story idea begins to take shape in his mind, and the scenes begin to fit into a pattern. Then the rearranging, the inclusion, the rejection of scene follows, guided hopefully by such a checklist.

The main idea for you is to begin writing and keep on writing until you have your story. Do not think of the checklist as a straitjacket. It is intended as a summary of the necessary disciplines described here and a guide to the organization of your scenes. And do not begin revision too soon; you cannot evaluate the story till it is ended. After the story has been written, then the checklist becomes a guide and reminder for the long process of revision and polish which every good writer discovers must be a part of the production of every good short story.

The Checklist

BEGINNING SCENE OR SCENES:

1. Is the deciding character reported in a statement which will be clear to the reader covering:

a. His governing characteristic with its phrases for repetition?
b. His problem?
c. His proposed solution?
d. His physical appearance reported and adequately repeated; age, name?
e. Is the point of view established?
f. Is the panoramic view reported adequately?

2. Do minor characters possess:

a. Characteristics which are clearly stated?
b. Physical appearance adequately reported?
c. A function in the story clearly stated?

3. Does the story begin at the causative situation, and is this situation clearly stated and developed in the report?
4. Is there a beginning of the development of mood and tone?

5. If the theme or idea is important, has it been introduced?

MIDDLE SCENES:

1. Are well-developed intensifications or interferences with the progress of the proposed solutions stated clearly?

2. Do the deciding character's decisions demonstrate clearly to the reader the functioning of his governing characteristic?

3. Has accident been avoided, or explained and used structurally?

4. Is the point of view maintained at all points?

5. Are mood and theme developed?

6. Is the End prepared for?

ENDING SCENE OR SCENES:

1. Are the results of the deciding character's decisions clearly shown?

2. Are the results inevitable or logical?

3. Are all loose ends tied up satisfactorily?

4. Is the idea clearly shown?

OF ALL SCENES:

1. Are all scenes necessary and in the best order? What about flashbacks?

2. Are other scenes needed?

3. Are transitions from scene to scene clear as to time, place, light, etc.? Are scene tags repeated judiciously?

4. Does each scene move the story forward, give insight into character and motive, lead to the final significance?

5. Is each scene adequately reported as to time, place, character, light, purpose, point of view, and the five senses?

DIALOGUE:

1. Is dialogue adequately used to develop and present:

   a. structure of the story?
   b. scene development?
   c. insight into character and motive?

2. Are the phrases accompanying the dialogue effectively used, successfully repeated, and properly positioned?

3. Is the dialogue accurately and properly idiomatic?

In the next part, Part Two, we will analyze three short stories in considerable detail, and comment specifically on the discipline.

PART II

Analyses of and Comments on Three Short Stories

In each analysis, the text of the story has been printed without interruption, with the analysis appearing in a parallel column, the paragraph beginnings of which match the points in the text under discussion. I suggest you read the entire text of the story first to become familiar with the story. Then a second careful reading of both columns, matching the comment to the point in the story, should make the analysis clear, specific, and concrete. Finally, the response to the appended "Ideas for Study" should be made as thoughtfully as possible.

"Granpa" and "So Young to Die" are written by students. "Granpa" was printed in Literary Cavalcade in May 1960 and reprinted in Bittersweet in 1962.

Story Analysis:

GRANPA
by Jeff Rackham

TEXT	COMMENT
I went to live with my grandparents on their farm in Missouri, just after I turned seven. I suppose at that time my Grandpa was not really old, but he seemed a terribly old man to me. There has never been a man with more wrinkles in his face than Granpa. They were not wrinkles of sorrow or anguish but happy wrinkles. They ran deeply through his cheeks and round his eyes and from the base of his ears down onto his throat and neck. He al-	*The first sentence establishes the point of view as first person subjective, "I" as the deciding character, his age (a most important item in a short story or essay without which nothing else can make true sense), and tentatively the causative situation, that is, the move to Missouri. It also begins the data on the panoramic view, for Missouri is specifically localized. This is a good first sentence. The rest of the paragraph reports the essentials about*

71

ways had a little stubble of whiskers on his chin.

the minor character, Granpa, very important for our interpretation of later scenes. There is a little more than physical appearance. The stubble and wrinkles, when repeated later, evoke this entire image of Granpa. There is development of insight into Grandpa's character with his seeming age and his deliberate neglect of shaving. Strong use of the sense of sight.

He farmed almost sixty acres with horses, not because he was a hard worker but because Granma was. I loved those horses. I watched him round them up in the morning and harness them, and I went to the fields with him and watched them all day long. They were beautiful to me; the largest one was grey and black and her name was Maud, the other black or brownish-black was Billy. Granpa never allowed me close enough to touch them because he said they weren't used to children, but more than anything else in the world I wanted to ride one of them. It didn't especially matter which one, although I think that secretly I liked Maud the best because she stood almost a hand taller than Billy, and her long shaggy mane hung way down over her forehead,

More panoramic view of the total farm, the field. "I loved those horses" introduces "I's" governing characteristic, repeats it, and leads clearly to the problem: "more than anything else in the world I wanted to ride one of them" states the problem succinctly. "I's" first solution is to ask every morning; the first interference is "No, not yet." Jeff uses here the familiar clash of wills and judgments. This paragraph provides some further oblique insight into Granpa in the first-sentence reference to Granma and a full report of the horses which are really minor actors. Maud is labeled, and we watch for later reference and meet it with the delight of recognition. Creatively the panoramic view in the first two paragraphs contains senses of sight and touch (implied)

and Granpa had to push some of it through the cheek strap of the blinders so that she could see. I asked him every morning if I could ride them, and he always said, "No, not yet."

One day toward the end of spring when the plowing was almost finished I went with him to the field and played around the fence and down by the creek, but finally it grew too hot; and I just sat in the shade of the hedge row and watched him and the horses.

I sat with my legs wrapped around the outside of the cool water jug and my back against the rough bark of the hedge row. The heat felt heavy and dense, even in the shade. The sun burned down, making the leaves in the wood on the other side of the field sparkle and flash.

Granpa still wore two pairs of overalls and a heavy wool shirt. He had looped the reins around his neck and pulled his broken straw hat down to his ears.

His great knotted hands gripped both handles of the plow, and he lifted himself into the air and pushed his weight down onto the plow. When he started the horses, he shouted, "Hey-ya!" and slapped the reins across their

and a long list of detail. Structurally, Jeff has reached the end of the Beginning.

Scene One: It begins the Middle of the story: time, (crucial here), place, light, and shade repeated, temperature, character, purpose, point of view. There are sight; touch: "cool water jug," and "rough bark"; smell; all elements but taste.

Note the insight into Granpa developed by his report of clothing.

Notice the sharp accounting for distance and perspective in the point of view as the team circles the field. Note the care with sequence.

backs, then "Gee-a-ther." He made all kinds of shouting noises as the horses plodded along bouncing him behind them. I could hear his cursing even when he trudged out of sight on the other side of the hill.

Two little sweat bees kept buzzing around me, and I swatted at them and finally killed one. I wiped the yellow puss-blood onto my Levis.

The horses appeared again on the other side of the hill, their great shaggy heads bouncing up and down against the crest of the earth. They dropped down into another hollow and I could see only the tops of their heads with their flickering ears and Granpa's hat bobbing along above the ground. Then their heads popped up and they strained back up the rise with Granpa joggling along behind, seeming to hold back as much as he could.

"May black boils seal the womb you came from, Maud!" he shouted. "Hey-ya! Hey-ya!" He stumbled and cursed. "Get in there, Billy."

I think that he wasn't really angry: he just liked to make noise, or maybe in that way he got even with Granma. He went round

The sweat bees help here, sound and touch mainly, but they effectively evoke a hot summer morning by connotation, which helps prepare us for the End.

Note how closely Jeff keeps his eyes on the scene, reporting the action in its time sequence faithfully and briefly, and building carefully to the final decision.

Granpa's shouting evokes distance and nearness. Further insight into Granpa again through the Granma reference, the need for this will be apparent in the final result. The problem and the governing characteristic are both repeated here with increased intensity.

At the end of this scene

and round the field cursing and shouting, and all the time I just sat and dreamed of the chance to ride those horses.

we return to the problem faced by "I."

Later in the morning he stopped them, yanked off his hat, took the reins from around his neck, and looped them over the plow handle. He came striding toward me across the furrowed rows of black earth wiping the sweat from his hatband. Sweat had turned his shirt dark across the shoulders.

I jumped up and held the jug for him. He stomped up to me smiling, hot, and dirty.

"Hard work, huh?" he asked, with his Southern slowness.

Scene Two: Though place doesn't change, the scene is new because of a new time, new (added) character, and new purpose. It begins with "Later in the morning" and ends with "Just you don't tell your granma": all dialogue and dialogue tag. Jeff makes no attempt to vary the "he said," or identifying clause. He relies on the phrases accompanying dialogue to bring the drama of decision to us.

"Yes," I said, and watched him hold the damp jug to his forehead for a moment. Then he removed the cork with his thumb, and with a motion of his arm, he flipped the jug into the air so that it rested on his elbow, and the water popped and gurgled as he drank. He finished and held it out to me. Water ran down the stubble of his chin. I held the jug with both hands and let the cool water wash around in my mouth and watched him smile at me. When I handed the jug back, I said, "Can I ride the horses today?" I tried to say

Note the long, fully developed accompaniment to "Yes," and its meticulous following of sequence of action in which the reader sees Granpa vividly and has considerable insight into "I." This is good reporting. It ends with a clean statement of the problem and its proposed solution. This time the suggestion succeeds, and the story moves into the Ending. Notice here how the senses are reported in dialogue. The accompanying phrases provide ample room for sense reporting: For smell ("hot, and dirty"), sound (voice,

it real casual and adult-like.

He started to smile, but then he frowned as he put the cork in. "Think you can hang on?" he asked.

"Oh, sure" I said, catching my breath and hoping.

"Well," he drawled, and wiped his face with his shirt sleeve.

"Please!" I begged.

"You're still pretty small," he said.

"I'm almost three and a half feet," I said, stretching myself slightly.

He shoved his hands into his back overall pockets and said, "On just one condition."

"O.K.," I said, feeling jittery and excited.

"Just you don't tell your granma," he said, and winked.

And I was off and running across the dirt. As I got closer to the horses they grew larger and larger. They were larger than I ever dreamed. I stopped about three feet from them and stared. They were so tall that I could have walked under them by just ducking my head a bit. They heaved and sighed and shifted and smelled like manure. Maud was all covered with white foam, and her hair was shaggy and falling out. Just as Granpa came up behind me she swung her head around and snorted at me.

"gurgled," etc.) sight, taste ("cool water wash around"), touch ("hold the damp jug to his forehead"), all reported in the phrases. You might learn from Jeff something about concrete verbs and verbals. This scene demonstrates how to use concrete verbs and climactic simple sentences with compound verbs. Take a good look. The scene sadly lacks report of light and change of light.

Scene Three begins the Ending: Jeff has changed slightly the time, place, and position, thus a change of scene; "I" has made his final decision regarding the solution to his problem; the rest is result, thus the Ending section. The vivid report of the team and of Maud in particular is produced by careful observation of a change in the position: "I" is now close up, not away across the fields. All the senses are in play here. Note the repeated phrase for Maud.

Her lips curled back, and she showed her greenish-yellow teeth and snapped them against the bit. I leaped back and Granpa caught me.

She rippled her skin and snorted again. I hung back in Granpa's hands, I wasn't so sure that I wanted to ride her now.

"Ready?" he asked.

"I don't think I'll ride them today," I said, trying to be calm. Maybe he didn't hear me because he caught my waist and lifted me up into the air. I grabbed his hands and shouted, "I don't want to, Granpa. I don't want to!"

"Nonsense!" he said gruffly and started to set me on the horse. I lifted my feet into the air and screamed.

"No, no, no, no, no!" I twisted and jerked and started to cry.

"You wanted to," he hollered, "so you're goin' to." He sat me on the horse, and I could feel the wet lather right through the seat of my pants. "Now hang onto the hames," he said, and placed my hands around the hot metal knobs. The sour-smelling sweat had darkened the bottom of the leather collar. I was terrified, and I was crying and screaming. Maud tossed her head, and I screamed louder. Her hair felt wiry and

The positioning of the speech and the accompanying phrases here is excellent. Notice how they illuminate character, motive, the change in attitudes as the solution progresses, the results of "I"'s decision rising to the cry, "I don't want to, Granpa." This intensification of the feeling from the relatively placid desire in the beginning through the active anticipation in the middle to the acute emotional pressure of the ending produces the desired heightening of suspense in the working out the solution. Note also the adroit use of abrupt break with intensity by the use of some humor: "'Well, goddamnit, let go!' So I did."

slobbery wet, and it stuck to my arms and hands. I hung on tight and closed my eyes.

"I don't want to, Granpa! I don't want to," I cried. I heard him walk to the plow and snap the reins. "Hey-ya!" he said.

I knew that I was going to die, and I pressed my knees into the horse and dug my fingers into the collar. The horses stepped off and I rose in the air and bounced. I started to scream, then I slipped to one side, and I grabbed and gasped for breath. I couldn't breathe, and I couldn't scream or cry, and I wanted my mother because she would have saved me. Then the horses stopped, and I felt his big thick hands around my waist. He lifted me away from the horse, but I was so terrified that I couldn't let go, and I still held on with all my strength. He pulled and yanked at me, then hollered: "Well, goddamnit, let go." So I did.

He stood me up in the dirt and knelt down facing me, and I opened my eyes. I gasped; my whole body shook and shuddered. The harder I tried not to cry the more tears ran down my face. I looked into his big wrinkled face and saw the grey stubble on his chin and in the groove of wrinkles.

In Scene Four, coming right after the sharp break, the tension subsides more slowly. Note the phrases here which evoke Granpa again and give credibility to "I's" declaration: "I loved this man more than anyone in the world," and all that follows.

The bushy black hair stuck out over his ears, and his lips were smiling slightly, and it was right then that I loved this man more than anyone in the world. He was my father and mother and grandfather and God and no one could ever convince me differently. I tried to stop crying while his eyes looked deeply at me.

"Now you listen," he said, solidly, but kindly, "You've learned something today that many people never learn." He rubbed his rough finger across my cheek and wiped the tear away. "You've found out that there are things in life that people think they want, but when they get 'em, they discover they didn't want 'em at all."

Note how Jeff puts the key sentence, in which he offers the final clear statement of the significance of this story idea, into idiomatic dialogue. This is intellectual insight of a high order. We see not only into Granpa but into the boy and the total experience.

I shivered and gagged on my breath again and looked at him. He stood up and turned me back toward the hedge row and slapped me on the rear. "Now take off," he said.

Scene Five, the final report, ends the story quickly and succinctly with a satisfying tie-up of loose ends.

I started stumbling back over the fresh black dirt still gasping and trying to stop crying. I heard him shout "Hey-ya!" and slap the reins. I turned and looked at him and wiped my eyes. The silver plow cut into the grey crust and rolled over the black earth.

"You granny-scratchin'

black-tongued mule!" he
shouted. "Get in there."

I walked on back to the
hedge row and sat for a
while, thinking.

Ideas for Study

1. Do you judge first person subjective to be the best point of view for "Granpa?" Why? Why not?

2. What is the intellectual significance of "Granpa?" Support your statement.

3. List some items of information Jeff must have been sure of to give this story its tone of authenticity.

4. Make a list of items you know about the character of "I" and Granpa. How were you made aware of these characteristics? How useful is dialogue? How does it illuminate character?

5. What is the best feature of this story? The worst? Why in each case?

Story Analysis:

The first person subjective point of view fitted the purposes which Jeff had in mind for "Granpa." But, as Fred Millett points out clearly in Chapter Three on point of view in Reading Fiction, *there are limitations to the use of "I." In the following short story Laurel Ellison chose to use the third person subjective point of view. In this story, therefore, the reader identifies with Linnie with no limitations on insight and with complete flexibility of scene. As you read "So Young to Die" be aware of the advantages of this third person subjective point of view and decide why it fits Laurel's intent. "So Young to Die" was printed in the May 1957* Literary Cavalcade *and reprinted in* Bittersweet, 1962. *Examine the story closely for structure as an art form, for creativity as sensory transfer of significant experience, and for its intellectual values.*

SO YOUNG TO DIE
by Laurel Ellison

TEXT	COMMENT

It was the sounds the mice made playing ball in the roof of the cabin that wakened Linnie. She yawned and began to work her way from the warm eiderdown softness of her nest at the bottom of the bedroll to the cold pillow at the top. Her skin prickled with the cold when she reached the pillow, and the button at the neck of her white flannel nightie was undone again, so Linnie buttoned it up, but it didn't make her any warmer. She reached down, pulled down her nightie and tucked her feet into its warm folds. Then she just lay there.

The bumping had stopped. "I guess even mice have to sleep sometime," she thought. She looked across the room toward the dim forms of her two sisters. Mart sighed and turned in her sleep. Robbie didn't move. Linnie wished the mice would start playing ball again. The cabin was scary when it was so quiet and dark.

She snuggled the top of the bedroll around her neck and lay there. She heard the springs of her parents' big

Scene One presents time, early dawn; place, a cabin bedroom; light, and darkness; and the senses of sound, touch (temperature, texture), and sight. Laurel has already identified all the main characters, given the sisters' names, and established Linnie as the deciding character, and the point of view of the story as third person subjective. She begins to suggest panoramic view with "mice" and "cabin" and "bedroll" and "canvas cover," all of which are associated with camping.

brass bed in the next room squeek. "Everybody but me's asleep." She twisted her head again to see Robbie and Mart. They were just padded lumps of darkness against the monk's cloth curtain on the window. It shone faintly, with the same glow that an egg has when it's held up to the light. She could feel the dampness of the air making the canvas cover of her bedroll clammy and stiff.

Mart didn't cuddle up at the bottom of her bed like Linnie did—any more. She used to, until last July when she had gotten polio and had hardly seemed to have enough strength to breathe, let alone move her small, tanned body. Linnie remembered when the doctor had driven up the mountain to the cabin to examine Martie, and how he'd said in his wheezy voice to Mama, "It's one of the less serious types of polio. Still, I'd like to make some tests." He hadn't looked at Linnie, and he didn't say good-by to her when he wheezed himself out of the door. Nobody even knew she was there.

Of course, Mama had been busy, and Robbie got to help her because she was two years older, but when Daddy had driven up each night in his green Forest

Scene Two is a flashback scene into memory reported within Scene One. Laurel makes the scene do hard work by supplying time, place, minor actor, sight, the sound in the dialogue with its attached phrases. She gives Mart her special characteristic (earlier illness) and Linnie her governing characteristic: (Nobody even knew she was there.)

Scene Three gives the relative ages of the sisters, very important always, and a neat report of Daddy, which also completes the data on panoramic view,

Service pick-up, he'd go right in to see Mart without saying hardly anything to Linnie. Then after dinner he'd write up reports that Linnie knew would go into the box marked LAND MANAGEMENT, CENTRAL UTAH. She wished Daddy would stop looking so tired and being so cross, that Robbie would stop acting so smart, and that Mama would let her in to see Mart.

even to the exact geography. Robbie is given her characteristic ("smart"); and the governing characteristic of the clearly emerging deciding character is repeated. Part of Scene One remains still in memory (flashback), but the necessary information leading to the causative situation is supplied.

Now Mart was better, but they still paid more attention to her. Linnie began to wonder if they even loved her any more. Nothing had ever happened to her to make them feel sorry for her.

This is transition to the present. It also clearly restates the governing characteristic ("Linnie began to wonder . . ."); the causative situation ("Nothing had ever happened . . ."); and the problem (how to be noticed); and it prepares for the suggested solution. This is a good, hard-working paragraph. Though it is narrative, it exists within Scene One.

Suddenly, Linnie sat straight up in bed. "I'm going to die," she said. The cold made her shiver, but she sat up anyway. "Dying is more important than having polio, and I'm going to die bravely." She said it twice but it didn't sound brave because her teeth were beginning to chatter.

Scene Four: With sharp report of sound and touch, Laurel here states flatly the suggested solution: " 'I'm going to die.' " This is good scening. It makes this one basic point of structure clearly and succinctly, and it comes immediately after the statement of problem. From this point on we are held in suspense, wondering whether the deciding character can solve her problem along the line laid down. Will the suggested solution work? In these first four short scenes the point of view, governing characteristic, causative situation, problem and suggested solution have come quickly and neatly in that order. In addition Laurel gave the characters with their characteristics, and the panoramic view to give reality and perspective to all succeeding scenes. Scene Four marks clearly the end of the beginning of the story. Also in this scene she establishes the tone of the story by juxtaposing " 'I'm going to die bravely' " against "her teeth were beginning to chatter." She repeats carefully throughout this technique of placing side by side the childlike tragedy against the ludicrous, to create the tone of good-humored, adult recognition of and indulgence of childish trouble.

She lay down in bed again. She could see the people at her funeral. They were all crying and saying, "She was so young to die. She wasn't even ten-and-a-half." Linnie could even see the beautiful little girl lying in a coffin made of cut glass and silk and lace. There was a sweet, gentle smile on the white, little face; and it was framed by a cloud of

Scene Five: The middle of the story begins here with a "dream" scene reported with sound and sight and with strong suggestion of light. The adjective pile-ups here sound childish, as they should. All the detail develops Linnie's problem, her suggested solution, and her governing characteristic.

shining auburn (not red) hair. Her mother came up and looked sadly at her daughter's smile and said, "She died so bravely," and her father had to hand her mother a dry hankie.

"I'd better write them a note," Linnie thought, "and tell them to put my 'Album of Horses' and 'Thee, Hannah' and 'King of the Wind' in my arms instead of flowers." She tried to make a hot, salty tear trickle down her face, but she couldn't cry, and her face began to ache from trying.

It was beginning to be light outside, although the cabin was still quite dark, Linnie could see the shadows that the rough place on the logs of the cabin walls made against the one below it. The whole inside of the cabin was painted gray, right over the logs. She liked them gray, because it made the red-and-yellow plaid of her coverlet show up more in the day. The bouquet of lupines and wild geraniums she had put in her window yesterday drooped from the edges of their bottle, silhouetted against the pale curtain.

Linnie wished Mart would wake up and talk to her. Maybe the mice knew. Maybe that was why they'd

Scene Six returns clearly to the present in the first six words of transition. Here Laurel attends to the changes in light and time and adds detail to the panoramic view. She uses sight skillfully, but she (sadly) omits the sense of smell. The governing characteristic and the solution are again repeated, for development.

Scene Seven is a transition scene, changing place and purpose, and reporting touch, sound, and sight.

stopped playing. Nobody plays when a person is going to die.

Linnie got out of bed and felt around for her red-and-white sneakers under the bed. They felt clammy and were colder, even, than the painted wood floor. She climbed up onto her squeaky old army cot again to put them on. Then she pulled the cheviot from the foot of the cot.

She slid off the bed, went over to the metal double bed, where Mart and Rob were sleeping, crawled over Mart to wake her up and sat down next to the wall. She patted Mart's tanned face, and Mart's brown eyes flickered open like the gas lantern's flame—and then closed. "Mart," Linnie whispered, "I'm going to die!"

"Everybody does, Linnie," Mart whispered back. "Do you want to climb in bed?"

"No," Linnie said.

"Be quiet. You'll wake up Robbie." Mart's brown Dutch boy cut didn't even look messed up, Linnie thought.

"Listen. Robbie broke her arm. Daddy's teeth got pulled out by that drunk dentist. Mama got pneumonia when she was little, and you got polio, and

In Scene Eight all the points of structure so far used are further developed. Note Laurel's use of the braid as repeated development of the deciding character's personality and her use of Mart, a minor character, to develop the story tone. Mart's age is established. Pay attention to Laurel's carefully reported sequence of action in her verbs and her transition. All the senses except taste are used here.

you're a year littler than me, see?" Linnie was pulling her right braid hard. She felt cold, now, and she unsnapped the side of Mart's double bedroll and climbed inside to warm herself. "Nothing bad's ever happened to me yet." Her eyes filled up with tears that made her braid look like a blur of orange watercolor. "See, God's been saving me up for the very worst of all, and what is worse than dying?"

Mart's eyes widened. "I'll bet you're right. I never thought of that." She lowered her voice and stared at Linnie. "When do you think you'll die, Lin?"

Linnie wiped her eyes with the sheet. "Today, maybe. Maybe now!"

"Well, let's go to sleep, then. We can't stop you." Mart snuggled down and put her arm around Linnie.

"No. I'll be back in a minute." Linnie climbed back out of bed, tiptoed across the floor, pulled the gray, wooden door open, and stepped out onto the strip of cement that ran along the east side of the cabin.

The sun hadn't come over the top of the sky line yet. She shook out the cheviot, wrapped it around her, and twitched her head to release

This is transition. Here is a good place to note the way Laurel has been using concrete verbs. "Climbed," "tiptoed," "pulled," "stepped," "ran," all evoke sensory impressions. So far in the story she has used the abstract "to be" forms only twenty-three times. Be aware of her verbs. They work without strain or ostentation.

her braids from under it. Then she started up the path to the latrine.

Small, rough stones looking like bit-off, hardened pieces of Mama's raisin pudding rolled under the soles of her sneakers and into the damp foxtails under the currant bushes. She pulled off some of the fuzzy, red currants that were still left and ate them one at a time. They were sweet and full of little seed grains. For the first time, Linnie looked down the mountain.

The whole valley was clotted with a mass of white and gray clouds; little wisps of pink-white vapor slipped along, close to the ground. Linnie didn't need to go to the latrine any more. She climbed up the three steps of the stile, pulled off the cheviot, dropped it on one of the steps, and ran down the other three.

She ran through the wet grasses to the middle of the field and stood there for a minute, then, forgetting she was going to die, spread her arms out straight and whirled. She whirled around as fast as she could in the mist, until her nightie was wet below her knees and stuck to her legs instead of whirling out as she twirled. She began to laugh, and she tossed her braids back over

Scene Nine supplies a transition in time, place, light, and purpose to the next scene which is intensely communicative, and very important for its empathy with Linnie.

Scene Ten: Knowing that the value of her story lies in its insight into the mind and spirit and sensory world of this little ten-year-old, Laurel has developed this scene fully. All senses are at work; all the elements of scene are invoked, the light and change of light, for instance, is reported six times. She keeps the tone; note the effect of the reference to the currants, for example. This

her shoulder and started to catch at the slowly-moving clouds around her. "I've never tried picking clouds," she thought.

Then she remembered— and stopped laughing. "And I guess I will never get to do it again." She turned and walked back up to the path. "It's too cold, yet, to be going without a wrap." She scolded herself, and climbed over the stile to get the cheviot and wrap it around her.

Then she sat down on the top step and looked down on the clouds in the fields and out across Philadelphia Flat. "Maybe that's what heaven's like," she thought, pulling the wet flannel away from her legs. The wet had made the little violet sprigs on her nightie go purple.

"Maybe," she said out loud, "maybe I'm in heaven now and don't know it." She hunched down on the splintery step and looked around her. She was beginning to feel really cold. Every summer when they came up here Mama called this place heaven. But this wasn't the right place, Linnie decided. In heaven they wouldn't have any flies at all, not even in the latrines. She straightened up and felt better.

Down at the foot of the stile a little yellow prim-

is a good place to call attention to Laurel's use of symbols. The closing of the yellow petals of the evening primrose becomes a fine symbolism of both little Linnie and the central idea of the death wish. Do you know enough psychology to define the meaning of such other apt symbols as "the warm eiderdown softness of her nest" in the first paragraph or, in Scene Seven, the wilted lupines and wild geraniums?

Note the verbs in this scene and study their sensory effect. Note the care with idiom in such things as ". . . the little violet sprigs on her nightie go purple," and note the accurate and minute observation.

Structurally Laurel has rounded out the death wish, Linnie's suggested solution, and given it reality and believability by accurate reporting.

rose was almost shriveled up for the day. Linnie watched it until the delicate yellow petals had formed a small, soft cone. "Now it's dead," she thought, "it only bloomed one night, and it's dead." She pulled her braid over her shoulder and chewed sadly on the tip. It tasted like Woodbury's shampoo and watery vinegar.

A quiet breeze had started to blow at the little wisps of clouds, and now they started to scuttle away toward the pale-green cabin. She stood up, wrapped the cheviot around her, and went a little way into the field. She held out her right arm toward the moving clouds. "I am a pioneer woman at my cabin," she said gravely. "I face a horrible death with bravery." Her eyes filled with tears. "Even pioneer women cried," she thought, and started across the stile and down the path, stopping to pick some more currants. "I may never eat wild currants again," she said, and went across the bridge and into the cabin.

She took off her wet nightie and spread it over the bottom of the double bed. Then she took off her red sneakers. She crawled over Mart and curled up

Scene Eleven is transition, returning from the moving experience of Scene Ten to the previous symbol of childish security in Scene Eleven.

beside her in the warm
bedroll.

At about ten o'clock that
morning, Linnie was sitting
outside the cabin on the
wood-cutting block while
Mama braided her hair,
when old Tim Mortenson
rode up on his bay horse,
Rachel. He wanted to use
the Forest Service telephone
that hung in an iron box
outside the cabin. Mama
had brushed Linnie's hair
until it was electric and was
flying around her face. The
sun shining on it made it
look like delicate threads of
spun copper. She wondered
if in heaven they made you
wear a cloth to hide your
hair like in the Bible. If
they did, maybe she would
go down into hell and see if
they made you wear one
there.

The sunshine silvered
Rachel's forelock, the hair
on her nose, and the long
stubble on Tim's tanned
face, intent as he cranked
the handle of the telephone
making three raspy short,
and two long rings, and
shouted into it. When he
hung up the receiver and
clanged the metal door of
the box shut, Mama invited
him to come in and eat
some of the newly-baked
cookies. She didn't offer him
any hot coffee, because Tim
was a very strict Mormon.

*Scene Twelve: Changes
of time, light, and character all reinforce Linnie's
problem and solution, but
no change in the problem
nor in the essential decision.
The succeeding scenes are
meant to increase this tension and maintain our suspense.*

*Notice that dialogue has
been used to develop either
character or structure or
scene. In Scene Eight it
builds chiefly structure; in
Scene Ten it permits insight
into the character and moti-
vation of the deciding
character; in Scene Twelve
notice how Mart's "Boy,"
offers insight into Mart and
by contrast into Linnie and
her problem. Notice also
how the dialogue reveals
both scene and character.
The essential thing to remember about dialogue is
that the words spoken and
their accompanying phrases
must both function in some
part of the structure.*

Tim chuckled from down in his plaid flannel shirt and raised his eyebrows at Linnie. "How'd you kiddies like to ride Rachel for a while?"

"Boy," Mart yelled from the doorway of the kitchen, "boy, we'd sure like to!"

Linnie let Mart and Robbie ride Rachel that morning. If she should fall off, she might die. Instead she sat down by Robin, Tim's best sheep dog, and looked for little sparkles on top of the mare's-tail clouds, in case the sun was shining on golden harps or something, in heaven. But she didn't see anything except two red-tailed hawks wheeling a lonely pattern in the sky.

That afternoon, Mama, Robbie, and Mart went down the mountain to do some shopping. Linnie stayed at home. Almost anything can happen to you in a car, especially on a narrow, winding road.

The scene is continued in place but there is a transition in time and some intensification of the problem.

She thought maybe she ought to say good-by to the mice, so she waited until the car had gone. Then she pushed through the tall grasses at the south end of the cabin and boosted herself under the eaves. She peeked in and whispered, "Good-by, mice." She couldn't see anything moving. She waited. Those mice weren't even paying at-

Scene Thirteen, transition in time. Note the intensifying repetitions.

tention; They didn't care
if she died.

When Mama and the girls
came back from town, they
brought Daddy with them.
And there was Robbie sit-
ting right next to him and
acting so smart. Linnie
wished she'd gone down
the mountain with them.
Then maybe she'd have gotten to sit next to Daddy.

After dinner, Daddy
brought out his guitar, and
they sat around the camp-
fire and sang. Linnie loved
this, and she leaned back
against Daddy's legs while
he played. She watched the
flames leap upward and
spit out little showers of
sparks when they reached
the blackness. They lit up
Mama's face and made her
hair shine as she sang, gazing all the while at the
blinking coals on the outside edge of the fire.

Beyond the warm circle,
the night was clear. The
stars seemed very close and
very white. Linnie turned
away from the fire to let her
face cool and to warm her
back. She shivered as a cold
breeze blew past her and
made the two tall, green-
black spruce trees sigh and
whisper to each other. She
could smell the raw green-
ness of bruised grasses and
the hot incense of the pine
in the fire.

Mart's eyes sparkled as

*Scene Fourteen evokes
rich experience with all the
scene elements; the sensory
report of lighting and touch
and smell are especially
effective, where intimacy
is to be evoked. Laurel
selects the sensory detail
carefully to build tension
and repeat the essentials of
structure. This scene ends
the middle of the story.
What follows, as the End of
the story, should report the
results of Linnie's decision
to solve her problem in her
own way.*

she sang. Linnie wondered if her own eyes sparkled. Maybe that was why Daddy liked Mart better. Daddy loved to sing Mexican songs, and now he sang about El Quelele, Linnie's favorite;

Papa White Hawk is dead,
Aye, yi, yi, yi.
He died at three in the morning.
And the baby white hawks,
Aye, yi, yi, yi.
Cry them to death in their woe.

Linnie's eyes filled with tears, and she could feel her nose going red. Everybody always talked about dying. She got up, kissed Mama good night, and then kissed Daddy. He set down his guitar and hugged her too tight. He set her down and kissed her on her sunburned nose. She was afraid maybe she would cry, so she said, "Good night, Daddy," and went into the cabin.

She undressed in the dark and got into her flannel nightie. She could still feel Daddy's short, rough whiskers against her cheek.

She was in bed when Mart opened the door stealthily and slipped in. Robin followed her.

"I told her about you dying," Mart whispered.

"Yeah, and you sure are a dim bulb," Robbie whis-

Scene Fifteen: If Linnie's governing characteristic is a sense of insecurity and neglect, if her problem is how to be noticed and cared for, and if her solution is to die and thus be made much of and cried over, the reader would expect to see the result (either success or failure) of the decision in this scene. Laurel has not made the results quite clear. The

pered. "Dying is the best thing that can happen to you."

"Jesus said so . . ." Mart interrupted.

"So," Robbie went on, "That's a best, not a worst to happen to somebody. And besides, you're still a baby. Nothing's hardly had time to happen to you yet. Besides, God doesn't save up people to let the worst happen to them. You only die because He likes you so much that He wants you to live closer to Him."

Linnie pulled her braid hard. Robbie was going so fast that Linnie couldn't interrupt until she stopped for breath.

"So that maybe you could go over to his house and visit Him sometimes?" Linnie whispered.

"Sure, stooge," Mart whispered back. Linnie bit the tip of her braid. It tasted like Woodbury's shampoo and watery vinegar. Suddenly she giggled. Robbie and Mart giggled, too.

After her sisters had gone to bed, Linnie was almost asleep when she was awakened by scatchings and scurryings, then a bump. She smiled and curled up again in her nest at the bottom of her bedroll. The mice were playing ball again.

dialogue of the last scene seems to report failure since there is no evidence that the parents demonstrated their love for Linnie to her satisfaction. But instead of having increased fears of insecurity, she allows her sisters to persuade her in the dialogue that her whole idea involved in the death wish was incorrect for her purposes; and she accepts the verdict happily and returns to her "nest," her problem not solved, but her frame of mind improved. This ties up the loose ends, but does not show a clear-cut result of the decision. Laurel may have felt an impending descent into sentimentality in the camp-fire scene and, wishing to avoid it, avoided also the happy direct result of decision. My own feeling is that the well-developed tone would have sustained a much closer adherence to structure. Perhaps Laurel should have reworked the last section of the scene and disciplined herself to structure.

Whatever you decide about the ending, you have seen an eventful day in the life of an insecure ten-year-old reported in fifteen scenes which moved forward in sequence to a preconceived significance. They held life in suspension, as does all good literature,

*while you realized some
aspect of its significance.*

Ideas for Study

1. Write a short paragraph identifying the panoramic view of this story. Be sure you stick to the text.

2. State Linnie's governing characteristic. What is her problem?

3. What is the tone of voice of this story?

4. What is the effect on tone of the adjective "couples" in the first paragraph of the middle: "She lay down in bed again. She could see . . ."?

5. What part of structure is "pulling her right braid hard"?

6. What is the meaning of the "nest" and of the "lupine" symbols? How do these meanings help tell the story?

7. Why is the "Tim Mortenson" episode necessary? Why not?

8. What is your judgment about the Ending of this story?

Story Analysis:

Let's have one more look, this time at a professional writer's work, before you try your hand at writing a short story. Kaplan's "Feels Like Spring" appeared first in The American Family *in 1952.*

FEELS LIKE SPRING
by Milton Kaplan

TEXT	COMMENT
I stop at the corner drugstore for breakfast of doughnuts and coffee. I eat fast because I'm a little late, and then I race to the subway station and gallop down the steps to catch	*In Scene One Kaplan establishes "I" as the deciding character, the point of view as first person subjective, and the governing characteristic of loneliness: "We're strangers"—this will*

my usual train. I hold on to the strap and make believe I'm reading my newspaper, but I keep glancing at the people crowded in around me. They're the same ones I see every day. They know me and I know them, but we don't smile. We're strangers thrown together accidentally.

I listen to them talk about their friends, and I wish I had someone to talk to, someone to break the monotony of the long subway ride.

As we approach the 175th Street station, I begin to get tense again. She usually gets into the train at that station. She slips in gracefully, not pushing or shoving like the rest, and she squeezes into a little space, clinging to the pole and holding on to an office envelope that probably contains her lunch. She never carries a newspaper or a book; I guess there isn't much sense in trying to read when you're mashed in like that.

There's a fresh outdoor look about her, and I figure she must live in New Jersey. The Jersey crowd gets in at that stop. She has a sweet face with that scrubbed look that doesn't need powder or rouge. She never wears make-up except for lipstick. And her wavy hair is nat-

be repeated. Panoramic view comes with "subway station." There are time, place, character, (no light, sadly), taste, smell, touch, and a first reference to the problem.

Here Kaplan states the problem succinctly: "I wish I had someone to talk to."

He presents the causative situation in a short sentence and repeats it later, with some insight into the deciding character. The minor character is reported briefly and given a characteristic: "graceful" "squeezes into a little space," "fresh outdoor look." The detail of the lunch in her envelope provides subtle insight. Note the care with which Kaplan reports details of "She": twenty separate concrete terms in ten sentences. Note how these are repeated. Far from static, this description moves the story forward to the result, sets up the first decision, provides clear insight into the governing characteristic and the problem.

ural, just a nice light brown, like the color of poplar leaves when they turn in the fall. And all she does is hold on to the pole and think her own thoughts, her eyes clear-blue warm.

I always like to watch her, but I have to be careful. I'm afraid she'd get sore and move away if she catches me at it, and then I won't have anyone, because she's my only real friend, even if she doesn't know it. I'm all alone in New York City, and I guess I'm kind of shy and don't make friends easily. The fellows in the bank are all right, but they have their own lives to lead, and besides, I can't ask anyone to come up to a furnished room; so they go their way and I go mine.

The city is getting me. It's too big and noisy—too many people for a fellow who's all by himself. I can't seem to get used to it. I'm used to the quiet of a small New Hampshire farm but there isn't any future on a New Hampshire farm any more; so after I was discharged from the Navy, I applied for this position in the bank and I got it. I suppose it's a good break but I'm kind of lonesome.

This paragraph states the characteristic of the minor character, and pairs it with the repeated characteristic in the deciding character. The problem is elaborated in a full paragraph of subjective report in which is reported, in addition, some details of insight, and the first proposed solution resulting from a decision.

As the development continues with some background of panoramic view which also helps develop into the deciding character, we have at the end of this paragraph all the essentials of the beginning of the story: Deciding character— his point of view, his governing characteristic, repeated phrases of character, the caustive situation, the problem and the first suggested solution with its built-in interferences: "She's my only real friend, even if she doesn't know it." The next paragraph begins the middle.

As I ride along, swaying to the motion of the car, I like to imagine that I'm friends with her. Sometimes I'm even tempted to smile at her, not in a fresh way, but just friendly-like, and say something like "Nice morning, isn't it?" But I'm scared. She might think I'm one of those wise guys and she'd freeze up and look right through me as if I didn't exist, and then the next morning she wouldn't be there any more and I'd have no one to think about. I keep dreaming that maybe some day I'll get to know her. You know, in a casual way.

The middle of this story presents a sequence of "dream" scenes, beginning: "I like to imagine," a little like the sequences in Thurber's classic of its sort, "The Secret Life of Walter Mitty." "I's" first solution, interfered with by the girl's indifference, changes now to the second solution: to dream the "real" friend. This paragraph starts a new scene in the story, Scene Two, with a new (dreamed) time and purpose. The paragraph also provides the transition into the dream scenes. Note that these are not flashbacks for information occurring before the situation arose. These scenes move the solution and decisions forward to the end.

Like maybe she'd be coming through the door and someone pushed her and she brushes against me and she'd say quickly, "Oh, I beg your pardon," and I'd lift my hat politely and answer, "That's perfectly all right," and I'd smile to show her that I meant it, and then she'd smile back at me and say, "Nice day, isn't it?" and I'd say "Feels like spring." And we wouldn't say anything more but when she'd be ready to get off at

Scene Three, new time, and intensified purpose. Be aware of the gradual rise in the level of intensity through the following scenes to the final emergence from the dream. This very necessary intensification of scene is developed by a clear use of repetition, and the careful selection of concrete details in the scene report. Dialogue is most effectively important here; study the speech and notice the accompanying phrases. They

34th Street, she'd wave her fingers a little at me and say, "Good-bye," and I'd tip my hat again.

The next morning when she'd come in, she'd see me and say, "Hello," or maybe, "Good morning," and I'd answer and add something like "Violets ought to be coming up soon"—something like that to show her I really knew a little bit about spring. No wisecracks because I wouldn't want her to think that I was one of those smooth-talking guys who pick up girls in the subway.

After a while, we'd get a little friendlier and start talking about things like the weather or the news, and one day she'd say, "Isn't it funny? Here we are talking every day and we don't even know each other's names." And I'd stand up straight and tip my hat and say "I'd like you to meet Mr. Thomas Pearse," and she'd say very seriously, "How do you do, Mr. Pearse. I want you to meet Miss Elizabeth Altemose." She'd be wearing those clean white gloves girls wear in the spring, and we'd shake hands and then we'd break out laughing and the other people around us would smile because people in the subway are so close

are very skillfully effective. Kaplan's use of the tenses seems flawless to me.

Scene Four. Study how "Violets ought to be," etc., and the accompanying phrases reveal character. How much can be realized about "I" from this simple disclosure?

Kaplan develops Scene Five fully to increase tension. Running through seven short paragraphs of dialogue, it moves the story forward according to a preconceived program of solutions decided earlier. At this point, answer some questions: why the persiflage about introduction? What is the effect of "clean white gloves"? (She might have been bare-handed). What insight into "I" is given by "I'd stand up straight and tip my hat"? One of the delights of this sort of subjective report is the recognition of self. We all daydream more or less constantly, projecting images of ourselves into dream situations. Perhaps we all skirt,

to you that they can't help sharing a little of your life.

"Thomas," she'd say, as if she were trying out the sound of it.

"What?" I'd ask.

"I can't possibly call you Thomas," she'd say, "It's so formal."

"My friends call me Tommy," I'd tell her.

"And mine call me Betty."

And that's the way it would be. Maybe after a while I'd mention the name of a good movie that was playing at the Music Hall and suggest that if she weren't doing anything in particular—

And she would come right out with, "Oh, I'd love it!" I'd knock off a little earlier and meet her where she worked and we would go out to dinner somewhere. I'd ask some of the men at the bank for the name of a good restaurant. And I would talk to her and tell her about New Hampshire and maybe mention how lonesome I got, and if it's a really nice place and it's quiet and cozy, maybe I'd tell her how shy I was, and she'd be listening with shining eyes and she'd clasp her hands and lean over the table until I could smell the fragrance of her hair and she'd whisper, "I'm shy, too." Then we'd both lean

more or less closely, the borderline of schizophrenia. Observe, too, the light-hearted tone here, poignant but not solemn, which the careful selection of detail produces, and which lends credence to the scene. Near the end of this scene is a tentative (dream) result of the solutions.

Scene Six reports a change of time and place. Senses work actively here. Note the use of smell and touch, both most intimate.

back and smile secretly, and we'd eat without saying much because, after all, what's there to say after that?

We'd go to the Music Hall and I'd get reserved seats and we'd sit there relaxed, enjoying the movie. Some time during the picture, in an exciting part, maybe her hand would brush against mine, or maybe I'd be shifting my position and my hand would touch hers accidentally, but she wouldn't take it away and I'd hold it, and there I'd be in the middle of eight million people, but I wouldn't be alone any more; I'd be out with my girl friend.

And afterwards I'd take her home. She wouldn't want me to travel all the way out. "I live in New Jersey," she'd say. "It's very nice of you to offer to take me home but I couldn't ask you to make a long trip like that. Don't worry, I'll be all right." But I'd take her arm and say, "Come on. I want to take you home. I like New Jersey." And we'd take the bus across the George Washington Bridge with the Hudson River flowing dark and mysterious below us, and then we'd be in New Jersey and we'd see the

Scene Seven brings the tension in the dream sequence to a climax with a full sense report which clearly states the (dream) solution: "I'd be out with my girl friend." The following narrative paragraph concludes the dream sequence of decision and solution and marks the end of the middle of the story. The reader is ready, now, to see how all this planning in the dream world succeeds. Arrival at 175th Street station begins the End.

lights of small homes and we'd stop in one of those little towns, Englewood, Leonia, Ridgewood—I looked them up on a map, wondering which one was hers—and she'd invite me in, but I'd say it was too late and then she'd turn to me and say, "Then you must promise to come for dinner this Sunday," and I'd promise and then—

The train is slowing down and the people are bracing themselves automatically for the stop. It's the 175th Street station. There's a big crowd waiting to get in. I look out anxiously for her, but I don't see her anywhere and my heart sinks, and just then I catch a glimpse of her, way over at the side. She's wearing a new hat with little flowers on it. The door opens and the people start pushing in. She's caught in the rush and there's nothing she can do about it. She bangs into me and she grabs the strap I'm holding and hangs on to it for dear life.

"I beg your pardon," she gasps.

My hands are pinned down and I can't tip my hat but I answer politely, "That's all right."

The doors close and the train begins to move. She has to hold on to my strap;

Scene Eight, "The train is slowing down," a clear scene repetition, returns us to the actual present. The repetition of the street station number tumbles the reader out of dream into reality and increases the tension: "Will it work," he says, "will the dream solution succeed?" This is the eighth and final scene. Everything that happens in this scene does so because it has been prepared for. It is believable because the reader has been conditioned, structurally, to believe it. The result of the series of decisions is clear success. All loose ends are accounted for. And the reader has progressed through a series of scenes to a significant realization of life, to a clarification, too, as one of our greatest tellers of stories, Robert Frost, puts it: "a momentary stay against confusion."

there isn't any other place
for her.

"Nice day, isn't it?" she
says.

The train swings around
a turn and the wheels
squealing on the rails sound
like the birds singing in
New Hampshire. My heart
is pounding like mad.

"Feels like spring," I say.

Ideas for Study

1. Explain the difference between a "flashback" and
the "dream scenes" in this story.

2. List the phrases and ideas repeated in order to
raise the level of intensity in the story. Show how at
least one of them operates.

3. Select five accompanying phrases of the dialogue
and show how they give insight into "I." List other instances of character development.

4. How does the item of the map of New Jersey give
insight?

Your assignment for Part Two: Write a disciplined
short story. Your world: family, home, work, school,
social contacts, your reading experience, the whole reservoir of sources available to you out of memory, brims
over with people in causative situations deciding on
solutions to their problems, and you are part of that
world. Communicate it in a disciplined report.

Some Useful Readings

1. Anderson, Sherwood, *Winesburg, Ohio*. 2nd Edition. Viking Press, New York, 1960.

2. Brondfield, Jerome K., ed., *Bittersweet*. Scholastic
Press, New York, 1973. This collection of high school
prizewinners demonstrates the high quality of work

done by young writers when they discipline their work into an art form.

3. Stegner, Wallace and Mary, eds., *Great American Short Stories*. Dell, New York, 1976. This is an excellent collection. Some of the stories referred to in Part One are here. Read especially "Silent Snow Secret Snow" and "He."

4. Updike, John, *Pigeon Feathers and Other Stories*. Knopf, New York, 1962. Paperback: Fawcett, New York, 1971.

PART III

Five Short Stories for Reading and Analysis

Preliminary Note: Part Three suggests that a beginning writer can learn how to write short stories by exercising rigid self-criticism in the writing of stories and, by reading competently written stories and analyzing them to discover technique, form, content, and so on. Part Three offers some help in finding good stories for analysis by reprinting five carefully selected stories, and by accompanying each with a set of questions and directions which should start and guide some analysis. The exercises are aimed at answering a central question: "What can you learn about writing your own short stories from reading and analyzing this one?" They are addressed to the learning writer, not to the literary critic nor to the student who reads for literary scholarship or appreciation.

A story derives from the writer's perceptive observation and careful report of scene and from structural discipline. A story represents an artistic observation and reformulation of life, reported within the discipline of short story structure. It is no exaggeration to say that you, as a character, and all about you, are at this moment facing actual problems, many of which will eventually arrive at a time when you will have to make decisions about solving them. School, family, social life, job, career, neighborhood, all offer problems. Many of them need, luckily, not be solved or can be held off indefinitely. But some of them will soon become *causative,* will demand solutions. All these are the raw material of short stories; all contain the central story idea: how to live in your own world in spite of family; whether to tell a lie or not; how to rise above the smug provincialism of your neighborhood; how to prevent cruelty to an animal; how and whether to test your own physical stamina, to prove yourself; or how to rob a bank. These are some of the story ideas which lie inside the scene reports and structural disciplines of the stories in Part Three. The stories all around you can become apparent to you if you will concentrate on creative observation and keep an eye out to structural disciplines. Story ideas are all about you in the raw material of life, but they do not come ready-made into stories. You have to discipline them, reformulate them, report them into the artistic performance of the short story.

I hope that reading these five stories, following the directions, and answering the questions in the guide to analysis, and going beyond this into individual analysis of further aspects of the story will be interesting work. I am sure it will improve your own writing of stories, which is our purpose.

The paragraphs of each story have been numbered for easy and accurate reference in working out the analyses. I urge you to be painstaking, to take time for careful study. My feeling is that it is better to analyze one story completely and correctly than to work on five of them superficially.

BUSH BOY, POOR BOY
by James Aldridge

"Bush Boy, Poor Boy" can demonstrate for you a good many points about how to make a short story. The question you pose yourself is always: "What can I learn about writing my own story by reading and analyzing this one?" I hope you keep this question in mind as you try to answer my questions and follow my directions on the pages following the story.

You may find useful some notes about the author, James Aldridge. He was born in Victoria, Australia, and grew up there and on the Isle of Man. A glance at Webster's Geographical Dictionary and at a map of Australia will show you how the Murray River borders northern Victoria and runs nearly 1,200 miles into the Darling River. It is navigable to Albury. Perhaps on some maps you might find "the town of St. Helen"; on mine it doesn't show. You might investigate the special connotations of the word "bush" in Australian geography.

"Bush Boy, Poor Boy" was copyrighted in 1951 and printed in Harper's Magazine.

I have numbered the paragraphs for easy specific reference, but you may need to number the specific line in the paragraph for exact analysis. I suggest you read the story through once for the initial experience, then reread as you analyze. Make use throughout of your checklist and definitions supplied in Chapter Eight.

1. Once there were two things that were worthwhile doing in life. One was to shoot a fox, the other to catch a twenty-pound cod. At one time these achievements were so important to me that I abandoned everything else in life to pursue them. Why, I couldn't exactly say, but the reason began somewhere in the difference between myself—a bush boy and a poor boy, and young Tom Woodley who was a town boy and a rich boy. There it began; but in the way of life, it became something quite different to me in the effort to achievement.

2. I lived with my father, a woodcutter, on the Murray River, three or four miles outside the town of St. Helen, Victoria. The truth is, I didn't know much about anything except the bush, whereas young Tom Woodley was a clever boy with everything he touched: school, playing sport, church-going, and being liked by everybody in the town, and that included the teachers and the policeman. Where Tom was the best of everything, I was the worst of it, except in the bush. Every boy in town had something he could laugh at me about, but once they came out of the town and along the river, I could beat them all: that is, until young Tom Woodley came out to the river in his father's Model-T Ford on a picnic and within an hour had shot a fox with a .22 rifle and pulled in a fifteen-pound Murray cod on a line.

3. These were things that I, a bush boy, had never achieved. I had caught amazing quantities of fish, and I had caught a Murray cod of ten pounds, but never anything larger. When I could get the ammunition, I had shot large numbers of rabbits; in fact, I almost lived by selling rabbit skins, yet I had never once been able to get a fox in range.

4. With Tom Woodley I knew it had been luck, but that didn't do me any good because I knew that I had

nothing to stand up to now, nothing at all; and I stopped going into the town altogether; in fact, I even stopped going to school, and I stayed in the bush, determined to catch a twenty-pound cod and shoot a fox before facing the laughter of the boys in shoes and the joking of men behind counters.

5. The fox was the more difficult proposition, and yet the day came when I was to stand near enough to a fox to club it to death, if only I had been big enough to do it.

6. It was really an accident. For once I was not hunting or fishing, but looking for mushrooms. I was on Pental Island, which was covered with lagoons and swamps and dry patches and clumps, and as I was walking through a shallow pool, I came out on a small dry rise with one clumpy bush on it. I was picking mushrooms under the bush when I saw the fox. He had smelled me, but there was nowhere for him to go. He was more afraid of the water than he was of me. He backed away from the bush, and I backed away from him. The dry land we shared was only about thirty feet square, and he was less than ten yards away; but here I was without a gun and there was the fox, standing with his tail up and his teeth bared, but not making a sound.

7. I stepped slowly back into the water. I couldn't do anything without a gun and I knew it would take me an hour to get home: I had to swim a river and then go over a mile through the bush. Even so, I knew foxes; and I knew that this one was terrified of the water and would die before he would move into it. So I put down the mushrooms I had collected in a sugar bag, and got through the pool and started to run for home.

8. At home I had a .22 rifle, but the very reason I didn't have it with me was my lack of ammunition; and as I ran I begged myself to think of a place where I could find just one shell: no more. As I ran I thought of the .22 shell I had lost last year in the woodpile. That was no good. I had tried a dozen times before to find it. I could not borrow any, and there weren't any shells in all the drawers in the house: I had searched them time and time before. I was running for nothing, but I

didn't stop. I ran through the high grass and came to the river. I jumped off the point and swam across the deep hole and waded the rest. Then I ran up the high bank, through the willow trees, and made for home.

9. I got home and started to hunt in the woodpile, raking up the chips with my hands and feet, still panting and puffing from the run. I couldn't find that .22 in the dust and the chips of a year ago, so I went desperately into the house. I looked in the chamber of my rifle, but it was empty: I had known, but I had hoped. Then I knew there was only one thing to do. My father was away cutting wood, so I went into his room and got the .303 that hung on the wall. It was so big that I could hardly carry it, but I lifted it down. It had a clip of three shells in the magazine. It was clean, but it hadn't been fired for years. My father wouldn't even fire it himself, and the shells were in it in case of emergency. I took it down and carried it outside. This was the worst thing I could do. I was not allowed to touch this gun, not to touch it at all. But I didn't care now.

10. I put the heavy .303 over my shoulder like a log and started to run back with it. I was tired already, and I was half-walking before I had gone far. Still, I kept running in spasms, I walked and ran, and when I got to the river I nearly sank trying to keep the gun out of water. I couldn't hold it up, and it was well dipped by the time I got across.

11. I covered the distance from the river to the lagoon very slowly. I was starting to shake inside, puffing in and out; but I managed to run the last hundred yards to the swamp and the pool. I looked across the twenty-five yards of water to the island, and at the same time I pulled back the bolt of the .303 and put a shell in the chamber. Then I waded across to kill my fox.

12. But the fox had gone. I kicked the bush and looked into it, looking for a hole or a warren, but there was nothing at all, except a few droppings and a feather. He had gone and that was that. I could understand how he had been caught on the dry land in the first place: a quick break in the lagoon had obvious-

ly flooded the land around him as he slept on the rise; that was clear enough; but I couldn't see how he could get off, knowing his terror of water. I started to hunt on the other dry patches, and then on the whole dry land. It was hopeless. So I went home with my mushrooms and the .303.

13. I got a hiding with a harness strap for taking the .303, because I couldn't give any explanation of why I had taken it. I did not try to tell the truth: I simply made up a long story about chasing a wild pig. My father said there were no wild pigs in the whole country. I knew that, too, but I got the hiding anyway.

14. I went back looking for that fox the next day and thereafter. I kept looking; and though I was eventually looking for any fox, it was always the same fox to me. I kept looking and hunting, even though I had no ammunition. Then one night I wept for a couple of hours in bed for the mystery and the difficulty of it all, and the next day I went back to fishing for a twenty-pound cod.

15. There were a number of places along the Little Murray River which were good for cod, and I knew them all. The best was at old Roy Carmichael's. Roy had a house which he had built of a boiler. Outside (near the river) there was a gate he had taken from some old church, but there wasn't any fence. On the gate there was a latch that said IN and OUT. Roy always put it on the right one if he was in or out. He had built mud steps down to the water's edge, and as the river rose in winter and went down in summer, Roy would mark the height on the steps with an iron peg. I used this peg to hold my rod as I fished for cod, and old Roy himself came down to get some water just as I was putting a mussel on a hook.

16. "Why don't you use worms?" he asked me.

17. "I've used up just about every worm in the countryside," I told him.

18. "What about the Council's pig yard?" old Roy asked.

19. "I can't go up there," I said. "I got caught digging under the stone floor."

20. Roy was thin and old. He had a gray mustache

that dropped right over his mouth. Sometimes he laughed for no reason at all, and he laughed now.

21. "How is your father, Edgar?" he bellowed at me.

22. "He went into town to sell some wood," I told him.

23. "How do you like it when they laugh at him in town?" Roy said.

24. I didn't know what to say to that, so I asked him why he lived in the boiler.

25. "I lived over it for twenty years," he said. "Now I live in it. That's the best boiler that ever went into a river boat. They don't make them like it any more. If she hadn't hit the Point, the old Rang Dang would be going yet, with that boiler still inside her."

26. I knew all about it. The old Rang Dang was a paddle steamer that had tried to come up the Little Murray. It had hit low ground at the Point and sunk. Old Roy had been the captain of it. He had waited around to try and get the Rang Dang up from bottom, but the boat had fallen apart, so he had only saved the boiler. He had stayed right there and lived in the boiler. That was a long time ago. I had asked him once why he didn't get another boat. He had picked up a dead sunflower and thrown it at me, so I hadn't asked him again. My father, Edgar Allan, had told me that he couldn't get another boat anywhere after that. They, I suppose whoever owned the boat, said he was drunk when he hit the Point. After that Roy never drank, just to prove that he had not been drunk at the time.

27. "You know that's a two-inch boiler," he said to me now.

28. "It looks thick enough," I said.

29. "It hasn't got a flaked spot in it. Come on up. I'll show you."

30. I had been through this before, but I hooked my rod under a stone and went up with him. He passed the gate and put it to IN. He opened the heavy metal fire-door and bent down to get inside. The boiler was filled with a number of things, mostly made from old petrol tins. It had a floor of wood and there were all sorts of clocks with bodies made of tins. There were flower pots in tins with curled-over edges, a cut-out tin

was set in a fireplace, and the bed was made of kerosene tins framed together. Everything was painted red. On one side, he had taken out a whole plate so that he could get into the extension he had built. You could still see all the holes where the pipes had been.

31. Old Roy gave me a sledge hammer. "Go on," he said. "Hit it. Hit it anywhere you like."

32. I didn't like doing it. When I hit, everything fell down from the shelves. He insisted.

33. "Hit it anywhere!"

34. I found a clear spot, gripped my bare feet on the floor, and swung the sledge hammer as best I could, upward. It bounced off the iron side, and everything rattled down.

35. "Harder!" Roy shouted. "Anywhere!"

36. I hit the side harder this time, in the same place.

37. "How old are you?" old Roy said. He was angry.

38. "Eleven," I told him.

39. "Can't you hit harder than that?"

40. "There's no room," I said.

41. "There has to be room," he said. "What happens if you're looking for a flaked spot and you don't hit hard enough? A head of steam hits it and the whole lot blows to smithereens. Give it to me. Look."

42. Old Roy swung the hammer up onto the plate. The whole place shook and the tins rattled. He hit it again in another place. Everything fell down and clattered about. Roy kicked everything aside and walked to the back and hit it there. He kept hitting it until he was too tired to do it any more.

43. "You see," he said. "Not a flake." He was shaking; he was an old man.

44. "What about everything on the floor?" I pointed to the mess.

45. "Junk!" he said. "The only thing worthwhile around here is the boiler."

46. We went out then and back to the mud steps.

47. "What are you fishing for?" he asked me.

48. "A big cod," I told him. "Twenty-pounder."

49. "You used to fish for bream."

50. "I know, but I'm after a big cod." And I told Roy about Tom Woodley and the fox and the cod.

51. "Have you been getting any cod lately?" I asked.

52. "No. Perch. That's all there is in this river. Yel-low-bellies."

53. "Fish are fish," I said.

54. "Why don't you go over to the Big Murray?"

55. "The river is still too high to swim."

56. "I'll take you over in the boat."

57. "No thanks," I said very quickly. Roy had taken me over once before, saying he would pick me up when I came back, if I shouted to him. I had come back and shouted, and he hadn't come. He had forgotten all about me. The river had been too high and fast to swim, so I had stayed on Pental Island all night, getting a hiding when I went home the next day.

58. "I'll come over with you," he said. "I'm getting sick of the taste of perch."

59. "All right," I said.

60. Roy went to get some lines and the oars to his boat. His boat was always tied up here at the steps. He had built it himself, and it was the best small-boat on the river.

61. Roy came down and looked at my rod and said: "What do you want a rod for? A line is better for cod: they are like elephants: they catch themselves."

62. "I like a rod," I said. I liked to fish with a rod. If I caught that twenty-pounder I wanted to catch it on a rod.

63. "Leave it behind," Roy said.

64. "It's all right. I want to take it."

65. Roy shouted: "Whatever-your-name-is, leave that rod behind!"

66. I stood there and didn't get into the boat.

67. "Are you coming or aren't you?" Roy shouted. He was red in the face.

68. "If I can bring the rod."

69. "Get in," he said. "Get in. Bring the rod. What do I care? You're like the rest of them. You can laugh at me! Get in. Do you hear me!"

70. He was shouting at the top of his voice, and he shouted and swore all the way over. As we went across we were carried downstream by the current, but Roy knew exactly where it would take him. He had another

set of steps on the Pental Island side of the river, and we landed right on them.

71. Pental Island was between the two rivers, the Big Murray and the Little Murray. The Little Murray came out of the Big Murray twenty miles upstream, it wandered about, then it came back to the big river just below Roy's place. There was a clump of gums where the two rivers joined, and that was where we were going now.

72. On the way I told him about the fox on the dry spit of land. I asked him what he thought had happened to it.

73. "Did you ever see a fox chased by a snake?" he said.

74. "No," I said.

75. "That's it," Roy said. "That's it, Edgar. He was scared off by a snake."

76. "If he wasn't scared off by me, he wasn't scared off by a snake."

77. "I tell you it was a snake." Roy got angry again. "They are more afraid of snakes than of you," he said. I didn't believe it.

78. At the timber we walked straight through to the deep hole under a hanging gum. Cod were always in the deep holes. Bream were on sandbanks. Perch were in backwaters. Fishing for perch you used a float; but for cod and bream you fished on the bottom, and used two hooks above the sinker.

79. "You can take the dead tree," Roy said. This was the best place. I thanked him, but it did not mean anything because wherever I fished, he would cast his line near mine and then come around by me and talk. He didn't believe that noise scared off the fish.

80. "Have you ever seen a fish with ears?" he used to say. When I said, "No," he would say, "Well how the devil can they hear? If they could hear they could talk, or bark. Have you ever heard them talk?"

81. "No," I would say, "but I've heard them bark."

82. "You're a liar, Edgar," he would say. "How can a fish bark? It hasn't any ears."

83. Now I walked out on the dead tree and sat on a fork. Half of the dead tree was in the water. I could

drop the line straight down into the hole; but I like to cast a bit. I baited with mussels, let about a yard of line hang on the end of the rod, put my thumb on the wooden reel, and swung the rod. The sinker flew out, taking the line; and it plunked down right where I wanted it. Roy undid a heavy cord line from a stick, baited it, and whirled it over his head and threw it. The bolt which acted as a sinker plunked down very near mine: too near. I jumped, because I believe noise frightens fish.

84. We sat quietly for a while, and I held the line lightly, waiting for bites. Then Roy got up and walked over to the tree and came out on it.

85. "Why don't you go to school?" he said to me.

86. "It is too far away," I said.

87. "School is never too far away," he said. "You could walk."

88. "It takes too long," I said. "Two hours."

89. "What are two hours! Can you read and write?"

90. "Yes," I said. I could read very little. I could hardly write. Most people thought I would say "No" when they asked me that, but I didn't like saying "No."

91. "That's not enough," Roy Carmichael said. "You have to know about figures and some history."

92. "I know," I said. "I would like to know about them."

93. "Yes. You ought to go to Castle Donnington school."

94. "I used to go," I told him, "but Miss Gillespie sent me home."

95. "What for?" Roy was angry straight away.

96. "She said I was pretty dirty; and I didn't have any books. It wasn't any good having them. I used to swim the river to save time, and I accidentally dropped the books in the river near the Point one day. They were no good when I got them up. It's funny she thought I was dirty: I had to swim the river every day."

97. "What does it matter if you're dirty? What's the matter with dirt? You know who the only clean people are? The drapers and butchers. The ones in the bank, and the dentists. You know who the best boys are at that school, Edgar?" he said.

98. "No," I said thinking about the fish.

99. "The little bleeders of the drapers and the butchers. Do you know what they grow up to be?"

100. "No," I said.

101. "Drapers and butchers. I've watched them. They are the ones for schools. The dirty faces can go to Hades. You can go to Hades. If I was a boy I could go to Hades. I am the only man alive who can take a boat up the Little Murray, but I could go to Hades. The ones that can sell a pair of drawers and keep their necks clean, they're the ones. If I had a boat, I would teach you to take it up the Little Murray. I'm the only man alive that can do it. What does your father do, Edgar?"

102. Roy knew what he did, but I told him: "He carts wood," I said.

103. "Is that a reason for a town to belittle a man?" Roy said.

104. I didn't care about that. I was getting small bites, nibbles. I could imagine the fish just pulling on the side of the bait, tearing it away without touching the hook, so I waited. Then it all happened.

105. "Look at your line," I said to Roy.

106. He looked over to the bank, and the willow springer to which he had tied his line had been pulled clean out of the bank, and was tight in the water. Before he could leave me, I felt a big pull—a tremendous pull—on my own rod, and I jerked it up to hook the fish; but the rod bent and nearly broke, and I knew I had my big one.

107. "You've hooked my line," Roy shouted in my ear. "You'll lose my fish."

108. "It's on mine," I cried back as I held onto the rod, almost falling into the water, just hanging on.

109. "No," Roy said. "You've hooked my line. Give me the rod."

110. He was dancing up and down, his face was red, and his hair was aloft. "You'll lose my line, you're pulling it in. You'll lose the fish."

111. I didn't have time to look around at Roy's line. I was trying to hang onto the fish that had hold of mine, and at the same time keep Roy from taking my rod away from me.

112. "What's the matter with you!" Roy said, and got a good grip on my rod. "Let it go, will you? I'll break it on your back."

113. The fish pulled, the rod bent, Roy and I held onto it.

114. Then Roy swung his arm and knocked me clean off the log into the shallow water behind, and by the time I got out he was reeling in the fish and walking back to the bank to land it. I ran over and tried to get the rod back, but he pushed me away and landed the fish.

115. It was a Murray cod all right, and it was more than twenty pounds. It was fat and gasping and kicking as Roy whipped it right up the bank away from the water. I ran up to get hold of the line. I could see already who had caught it.

116. "It was on my hook, it was on my line," I cried at Roy, and I was really crying. "You caught my fish." It had been Roy's line that had tangled with mine: it was his that had ruined this catch. "You caught my fish," was all I could shout at him.

117. "What's the matter with you?" Roy said, and I thought he was going to hit me again. "I got the fish out, didn't I? You would have let it go, you would have fallen in the hole, you would have lost it."

118. "You got my fish," I said. "That's the fish I've been waiting to catch."

119. "Well, you caught it," Roy said and put his foot on the cod to take out the hook.

120. "I didn't catch it," I said, "You did!"

121. "It was on your line," he said. He was laughing now.

122. "What's the good of that! You pulled it in. You caught it. You took it away from me. You caught my fish."

123. "Well, you can have it," Roy said.

124. "I don't want it. I just wanted to catch it."

125. "Well, you caught it. You can say you caught it. I won't deny it."

126. "That's no good," I cried. "Tom Woodley caught his fifteen-pounder. You should have let me catch this one." I was not exactly howling, but I was

practically screaming at Roy, because I knew that I would have little or no chance of ever again catching another big one.

127. Roy was sorry and said: "Never mind, Edgar."

128. I swore then, round and long.

129. Roy got mad again and threw a clod at me.

130. "You stole my fish," I said from a distance, to insult.

131. "Take your fish!" he shouted.

132. "I don't want it," I said, and then I ran.

133. I tried to get Roy's boat out and back across the river, but I beached it on some shallows and Roy caught me and took it over and laughed at me all the way across. Then he held onto me, on the other side, and I said I'd never get a fish like that and never get a fox. Never again. I was finished now, and Roy knew it, and he hung onto me and told me he would let the world know I had caught that fish; and moreover he would help me get that fox. He had ammunition and a fox whistle, and if I came back tomorrow he would hunt a fox and maybe fish again. Then he let me go.

134. "Don't you want your rod?" he called after me as I went.

135. "Keep it," I shouted back, and swore at him again.

136. He threw it at me, and I ran away cursing and shouting, leaving my rod, and leaving the big Murray cod that should have been mine.

137. That cod was mine, and I knew it. Yet not having it, and not having caught it, the thing began to overwhelm me. It was always on my mind, from the moment I lost it, and before long it had become something that I had but could never have: something I had achieved yet could never achieve. The puzzle and mystery of this was even worse than the mystery of the disappearing fox, and if I'd wept a little in bewilderment over that, this time I had nightmares that made terror of incidents I had long since forgotten. All of them were puzzles, and all of them were repetitions of the same feeling: to have wanted something so much, to have almost had it, and then to have lost it at the moment of success. It made me sick, and it seemed that I was

never in peace again. More and more the necessity of killing that fox became a way to solve these things and give me back a day without thought and a night without terror. That fox was the fulfillment somehow, and I knew I had to achieve it or be miserable forever.

138. Then late in summer Roy gave me my chance. He found me one day on Pental Island, and after he had boxed my ears for taking a revenge shot at his fox terrier, he began to laugh at me.

139. "Are you still bawling and howling about that fish?" he said to me.

140. I hadn't forgiven him even then for that fish. He had certainly told the town I had caught it (a twenty-eight-pounder), and he had thus half-saved me from Tom Woodley and the town boys; but I hadn't forgiven him because I knew I hadn't caught it, and because my sudden nightmare and its life-puzzle wouldn't let me go, and I blamed him for that, too. I wouldn't talk to him about that fish, but he laughed and didn't care, so I didn't care, and I told him I would call the next day and get my rod back.

141. "Do you still want that fox, Edgar?" he asked me.

142. "Yes, but I want to get it myself," I told him.

143. "Don't be such a moaner," he said. "And if you do want a fox, you come down here tomorrow morning before daybreak and I'll show you where you can get one."

144. "Where is he?" I asked Roy. I didn't trust him now.

145. "You come down tomorrow morning and I'll show you," he shouted.

146. "You'll show me where it is, and then you'll shoot it yourself," I said.

147. "You holy little beggar boy," he called me with a red face. He seemed very upset, and I was sorry. "You come down here tomorrow morning before light and I'll take you over and get you that fox! D'you hear!"

148. "All right," I said, because he seemed desperate about it.

149. I don't think I slept at all that night, because

I knew that Roy would really show me a fox, and within shooting range. By now, hunting the fox had become habit, even though it was still the most vital thing in my life—the one solution and the one satisfaction to the puzzle and inconsistency of each day and each thing. I just didn't know where I stood these days, and more and more all things had become a puzzle to me because of the loss of that cod. Perhaps it was my own doing now, because I could always set off on a blind and hopeless route of thought by asking a few questions about myself, and then about anything: a worm, a gatepost, a hinge, a piece of wood. All I had to do was look at anything and ask myself what it was and where it came from and what had brought it to this state and where would it go, and all the nightmare of the lost Murray cod would return. Yet on this night I knew it would end, because tomorrow I would hunt that fox, shoot it, achieve the simple aim, finish this whole puzzle, and go back to normal again. That was tomorrow.

150. I was over at Roy's long before light, and I had to kick on the boiler door to wake him up. He told me to go away and leave him in peace, but I kept on kicking the door and he finally got up. He gave me a piece of cold meat to eat, and we rowed across to Pental Island. Roy knew Pental Island even better than I did, because he had trap-line all over it, and he covered it almost every day. We emptied a few of his traps as we went, and he had me carrying the rabbits on my shoulder as he walked ahead.

151. "Don't make so much noise," he said to me as we climbed a little hill. The rabbits were hitting my back, and their bellies were making a rolling and rumbling sound. "Drop those things and keep quiet," he said in a whisper.

152. Roy didn't creep, as I would in hunting. He walked upright, but he walked very carefully and slowly, stopping absolutely still from time to time and then moving on again. I moved behind him, doing what he did, and holding my .22 loaded and ready. When we reached the dry red top of the hill, which was bare and round, Roy lay down carefully and put his head over the top. It was still dark, but light was breaking the sky.

153. "Down there," Roy whispered and pointed to a clump of three or four sphinx bushes, "is a fox warren. That old fox is sleeping there now."

154. "I can't see him," I said.

155. "Of course you can't," Roy growled between his teeth. "He'll be coming out when the sun comes up. Can you hit him from here?"

156. It was about fifty feet down to the clump, and if the fox wasn't running I knew I could hit him. "Leave him to me," I said because I didn't want Roy to interfere. He had a .22 himself, and he held it ready for use.

157. "Well, keep your mouth closed and your feet still," Roy said, "and wait; and when you see him come right out, let him have it."

158. We waited, and I had a feeling now that this was all right. It was simple enough to be lying here, it was simple enough for anything in life at all. The sun would rise, the fox would come out, I would shoot, and life would again be normal. I had never felt so sure and relaxed in my whole life before, and I looked at Roy and cocked a grin. I was forgiving him the cod.

159. "Keep your eye on that bush," Roy whispered angrily.

160. I watched the bush and watched the horizon. The sky became pink, the mist rose, the crows flew high, and the kookaburras laughed; and then came the sun; and a little after the sun came the fox.

161. He was old and red. He had white feet, a white tip on his tail, and alert ears. He came out of a hole near the bush and put his head around quickly and lifted his nose up and crouched. Then he walked a few feet as if the ground was hot right under him. He turned around and looked straight up at the hill; and then he sat on his tail and licked his paw, and I had my rifle up to my face.

162. My .22 was old and the sight was off, so I sighted below and to the left of his head. It was easy and sure. The chance was here, the world was assured, and just as he licked the side of his jaws, I was easing on the trigger.

163. Yet I didn't fire. Whatever the reason, what-

ever the restraint, I didn't want to kill that fox and I
didn't intend to. I held the sight and kept my cheek on
the gun and the finger on the trigger and thought to
myself that all I must do is give it a pull and that fox
would be dead, and I would be alive.

164. "Go on," Roy said as if he would kill me himself for being a fool.

165. "I don't want him," I said and put down the
gun.

166. "Shoot!" he said right in my ear.

167. "I don't want him!" I said aloud and the fox
heard and was gone like a shot. Roy stood up and I
could see his .22 follow the fox for the first few seconds.
Then he fired. I was still lying down, but I saw the old
red fox go tumbling over; but I didn't care. At the same
moment another one came leaping out of the warren
and went running away, full of life.

168. "Why didn't you shoot!" Roy cried as he re-
loaded his gun.

169. "I don't know," I said. I really didn't know.

170. "Are you sick or something?"

171. I shook my head. I thought for a moment that
I would like to stay on this hill forever.

172. Roy looked hard at me and laughed for no
reason and forgot about the fox and sat down on the
side of the hill.

173. "How old are you, boy?" he asked.

174. "Twelve now," I told him, still waiting for his
temper.

175. "Twelve," he said slowly. "Do you know how
old I was when I lost the Rang Dang, lost my boat,
lost everything, and never got it back?"

176. I didn't know and I didn't care.

177. "Fifty-two," he said. "Fifty-two."

178. I had no idea what he was talking about except
that he had lost something and never got it back. For
my part I only knew that I was quietly happy again
without knowing why.

179. If I had hoped to solve the puzzle of life by
killing a fox for the loss of the cod, I knew I was
wrong. Life was life, somehow, and that fox had been
too alive for me to shoot. The fish didn't matter, the fox

didn't matter, Tom Woodley and the town boys didn't matter; and though I had spared one life to learn so much, I had killed five or six rabbits by the time we went home.

180. Yes, life was life; but I had it licked.

Guide to Analysis

A. SCENES

1. There are twelve scenes and seven narrative transitional sections. Can you bracket each of those scenes and narrative sections? Remember: a scene exists in a *particular* time and place, etc.

2. Select the scene you can "realize" most fully and elaborate the eleven components. Go as far with this exercise as you like.

3. What paragraphs comprise the essential panoramic view?

4. What can you learn about the handling and the uses of panoramic view within scene in paragraphs 70 and 71?

5. Explain fully how specific names of things give authenticity to this story. For examples, examine paragraphs 41 to 78.

6. Is this production of authenticity equally true of "drapers" and "bleeders" in paragraphs 97 to 101?

B. STRUCTURE

1. What specific elements of structure does Aldridge supply in the first paragraph? In the entire panoramic view? How many times has he tagged the problem in the panoramic view?

2. Why did he write the last sentence in paragraph 1?

3. Describe the point of view in this story. In what sentence is this duplicity of tone first made clear? Did you note any deviation from this point of view? How does the tone help to produce the humor? Where?

4. Here is a rough outline of the story structure. Indicate, after each part, the sentence (using numbers of paragraph and sentence) which first indicates that structural part:

I. The causative situation:

II. The deciding character:

    a. his governing characteristic:

    b. his problem:

        his *first* solution:

            the *first* interference:

        his *second* solution:

            the *second* interference:

        his *third* solution:

            the *third* interference:

III. The result:

5. How many times (count) did Aldridge repeat the basic characteristic and the problem?

6. At what exact points can you mark the end of the Beginning; the end of the Middle?

7. How can Aldridge defend his "result"?

    a. Is it prepared for? (specific lines)

    b. Does it result from: the governing characteristic? (specific lines) the solution suggested?

8. Why are paragraphs 6 to 8 of Scene One necessary?

9. Why are the materials in the long transitional narratives of paragraphs 8, 10, and 11 not reported in scene?

10. Why does the story require the boiler episodes of Scenes Six and Seven, paragraphs 26 to 45?

11. What insights into the boy do we get in the narrative of paragraphs 133 to 137 and in 149?

12. What can you learn in these paragraphs about transition (as distinguished from scene report) in carrying out the story structure?

C. DIALOGUE

1. Study the dialogue in Scene Ten (for example), paragraphs 79 to 132. Some critics have called this dialogue "naturalistic," as different from "artistic" or "realistic." What characteristics here would you label "natural"?

2. Read Roy's dialogue in paragraphs 173 to 177.

What insight into his character is supplied here? Point out specific spots in the story which have prepared us to accept this insight near the end. State Roy's governing characteristics.

3. What insight into the boy do we get in the narrative of paragraphs 133 to 137? Why did Aldridge use narrative here instead of scene report?

4. Explain the consequent order of dialogue tags as used by Aldridge. A good example might be the passages from paragraphs 153 to 157.

D. THE STORY IDEA

1. How is this story a significant clarification of life?

2. The story idea is summed up in paragraphs 167 to the end. State it.

3. Show the specific lines which tag the story idea from paragraphs 1 to 167.

WULLIE

by Howell White

Howell White has been an engineer, a technical writer, a purchasing agent, and a part-time writer of fiction. "Wullie," which appeared in Cosmopolitan *in 1958, won the Maggie Award that year.*

The point of view in "Wullie" is interesting for several reasons. "I," though he is the teller of the tale, is not the deciding actor. He is simply the reporter. The events merely happen before him, and he reports them using the third person objective point of view. But the fact that this is an eye-witness report insures credibility. Further, we can get more than ordinary insight into Billy (the deciding actor) because Joe knows him intimately. In a way, Joe's obtuseness sharpens our own insight. Study how this is accomplished; for example, in Scene One, paragraph 16, the question is revealing of both Joe and Billy.

The story has a very strong ending, brought about partly by the final dramatic act and partly by skillfully intensified scene report through the Middle of the story. This skill in building intensity is worth careful study.

1. It is almost too good to be true to wake up on a Saturday morning—no school—with a shiny new .22 rifle propped against the bed, and with the ground white with the first snow. When you're twelve, happiness comes in big chunks.

2. I carried the gun downstairs and held it in my lap while Mom brought me ham and eggs as if I were a king. When you're twelve you're too old for a regular birthday party with cake and ice cream and girls in party dresses; but the day was mine, and I knew just what I wanted to do with it. In fact, I already had something cooked up with Billy Ryan. As soon as I finished breakfast, I phoned him.

3. "I got it, Billy," I told him. "It's a beauty."

4. "That's nice, Joe," he said. "Did you see the snow?"

5. "Oh, sure," I said. "We're going to the quarry, remember? And I'll teach you how to shoot."

6. "Say! It'll be beautiful with all the snow."

7. I was a little disappointed that Billy was more excited about the snow than about my new .22. Billy was my best friend, but I couldn't always figure him out.

8. Billy had moved to Woodfield the previous summer from some place in Arizona. His Dad worked for a big company with plants and offices all over the country, and he was always being transferred. Besides Arizona, Billy had lived in California, Kansas, Chicago, and in Atlanta, Georgia.

9. It was quite a contrast to my life. I'd never lived anywhere but Woodfield, and neither had my parents. My dad owned the department store on Main Street—the one with the big red and gold sign that looked like a five and ten.

10. It was only a short walk from Billy's house, and he was over in ten minutes flat. That was just enough time for Mom to make some sandwiches. We put the sandwiches in our pockets; Mom patted us on the back; and we were off. I carried the gun, muzzle down, under my arm the way Dad had shown me.

11. We swung off up the main road, not saying much, just covering ground until we got to the old Peabody farm. We turned off the road, scrambled down the bank

and then climbed over the old stone wall into the pasture. Here we picked up the old road that led to the granite quarry.

12. There wasn't too much snow, so walking was easy; and there wasn't a cloud in the whole blue sky. The air was cold, stinging in the nostrils, but the big yellow sun kept us warm. On the open fields the snow was so bright that if you looked at it too long, little red and green specks would start dancing in front of your eyes.

13. "Hey, look!" Billy cried in sudden excitement. "A fox!"

14. I brought up the gun in a hurry. "Where?" I asked.

15. "Oh, no!" Billy said. "Don't shoot anything."

16. "What good's a gun if you don't use it?"

17. "Oh—please! I don't want you to shoot anything." He was looking at me, eyes wide open, kind of half scared. "Please!" he said again.

18. "All right." I dropped the gun. "Didn't see him anyway."

19. "I didn't see a fox," Billy said, "just his tracks. Look!" He pointed to the snow. I saw nothing to get excited about.

20. "He stopped here for a while. Maybe he saw something. Yes!" Billy was ranging in the snow. "Over here, a rabbit. We can reconstruct the crime." Billy took a long step, careful to avoid the tracks. "The fox jumped . . . the rabbit made two hops . . . and the fox caught him, here! See, there's fresh blood in the snow."

21. "Let me see."

22. "Come on, let's see where he went!" Billy was off like a tracking dog. We followed the trail in the snow for half a mile and then lost it in the pines by the old Indian well.

23. "Well," Billy said, "I guess Mr. Fox will have his meal in peace. Now—where do we go from here?"

24. We would have to walk a good mile to the quarry if we went back the way we had come, but there was a shortcut that would take us past Rafe Jones's place. Rafe might not even be there. And if he was, we could probably sneak by without being seen.

25. As we went along, I told Billy about Rafe. Ever since his wife died, he had lived alone in a shacky old farmhouse that was falling down around his ears. He kept some chickens, and made enough from them to keep himself in canned goods and have enough left over to get drunk every Saturday.

26. Nobody liked Rafe. He was a really mean person. Just about the meanest thing he ever did was back when he still had his egg route, and he set out to cure the Bements' little dog of chasing his truck. Nobody could blame the dog for chasing that beat-up truck of his; it rattled and clanked and moaned and groaned and it smelled of chickens and Rafe. Well, even though the Bements were just about Rafe's best customers, he stopped the truck in the road before he turned into their place, and he tied a burlap sack to each of the front wheels. Then he drove, flip-flap, flip-flap, down the long drive. Skippy, the little terrier, made one dash at the flapping sack, sunk his teeth in it, and then was spun off violently as Rafe stepped on the gas. Rafe Jones was mean, clear through.

27. When we came in sight of his place I was relieved that his old truck was not in the yard. Rafe was probably in town, starting to tank up. The old place hadn't changed much since I'd seen it last. The roof sagged a little more; a couple more windows were broken, maybe. The same old cans, bottles, and bits of garbage lay around the front door. There was one new thing . . . a big sign nailed to the maple tree next to the chicken house: KEEP OFF—BAD DOG. And there was the dog, chained to a trolley that ran between two trees, across the front of the chicken house.

28. He was the ugliest dog I'd ever seen. The minute he caught our scent he put his head down, his hackles went up, and he charged toward us with his blue lips pulled back from yellow teeth. When he reached the end of the trolley, the chain caught him and snapped him to his hind feet. He stood there, fighting the chain and snarling.

29. He was a big brute, of no particular breed, but he must have had some mastiff in him, and maybe some

German shepherd. His coat was rough, shaggy, kind of a dirty orange-brown in color, with some bare pink spots on his haunches where the skin showed. He had flapping ears and a mangy sickle tail that drooped down between his legs.

30. The dog fell back. Then, tongue flecked with foam, he charged again. The chain jangled as it came straight, and the overhead trolley squeaked against the eyebolts.

31. "Let's get out of here," I said. "I don't want to be around when that thing breaks."

32. I started on, but Billy did not move. He was standing facing the dog. Without turning, Billy said softly, "Go on, if you want to. I'm going to make friends."

33. "Don't be crazy. That dog's mean. You read that sign?"

34. Billy never turned. "Be quiet," he said to me. "Go or stay—but don't make a sound."

35. I stayed, my heart in my throat. Billy stood, not moving, for ten, maybe fifteen minutes. The dog was now tired out. He stood there, head drooping, hackles raised. Billy talked to him in a sort of croon. I couldn't hear the words, just the tone. Then Billy moved a step closer to him. The dog snarled deep in his throat. Billy wheedled softly. The snarl died. Billy took another step forward, and another, and the dog eyed him. Billy reached out his hand, holding out the back of it. He was near enough so the dog could have sprung at him. It was comforting to have my gun along.

36. But the dog didn't jump him. Instead he started to sniff the back of Billy's hand. Billy let him sniff all he wanted, and all the time Billy was crooning to him. Next thing I knew he was in close. The dog had his nose to Billy's trousers, sniffing. Every once in a while Billy took a slow step toward him. When he reached an overturned bucket, he sat down. The dog stood near him, head down, hackles still up. Billy's hand slowly went out to the dog's shoulders and Billy began to stroke the angry hairs, talking, talking all the time. Gradually the angry hairs lay down.

37. Then everything seemed to happen at once. Rafe's truck rattled past me and skidded to a stop by the maple tree. Rafe jumped out, shouting, "What the hell's goin' on?"

38. The dog turned on Billy, slashing with yellow teeth. Billy jumped from the bucket and ran beyond the reach of the chain. The dog charged at Billy but the choking leather collar snapped him upright, and he stood clawing the air.

39. Rafe's face was splotchy red. "Get off'n my place!" he shouted over the dog's raging. "And don't come back."

40. He took a bottle from his pocket and tipped it to his lips to drain it. "Aw, shut up," he shouted at the dog, and hurled the bottle. It was a wild shot but lucky. The heavy bottle caught the dog on the head. He did not yelp.

41. We took off, I tell you.

42. I had always liked the quarry in the wintertime. The straight, granite walls curved like a cup; they reflected and held the sun's heat like an oven.

43. I found some old cans and set up targets against the granite wall. Between Billy and me, we shot up two boxes of cartridges. Then we took off our coats to feel the sun while we ate. I stretched out on a rock. "This is the life."

44. Billy sat up, frowning. "What are we going to do about Wullie?" he asked.

45. "Wullie?"

46. "Red Wull. Rafe's dog."

47. "How'd you find out his name?"

48. Billy laughed. "Oh, I don't know what his name is. That's just what I called him. He seemed to understand."

49. "Oh," I said, "I get it now. Wullie, like Adam McAdam's Red Wull, the killer in Bob, Son of Battle."

50. "No!" Billy was fierce. "He wasn't a real killer. He just never had a chance."

51. "I never thought of it that way. I always thought that he was the bad 'un."

52. "There aren't any bad ones," said Billy. "Did you see those sores on Wullie?"

53. "On his back? Looked like mange."

54. "I don't mean those. Around his neck where the collar is, it's all raw and open. There's pus in it."

55. "I didn't get close enough. Say—let me see your hand." I had forgotten about Billy's hand until that moment.

56. Billy opened his hand. There were two scratches on his palm. "It's nothing. I sucked it clean."

57. "Better put something on it."

58. "Oh, yes. Say—" Billy was suddenly excited. "I'm coming back tomorrow. We've got some wonderful salve, penicillin stuff. I'll put that on Wullie's sores."

59. "We can't come back."

60. He looked scornful. "You don't have to, if you're afraid."

61. "I'm not afraid," I said loudly. But I was lying.

62. We shot up a couple more boxes of cartridges. By then the sun was dropping so we started home.

63. We didn't talk after we'd decided to come back to see Wullie again. And there was no talking Billy out of it. Billy didn't even notice the tracks in the snow on the way home. He just slogged along, thinking about Wullie.

64. We had just come into the cedars near the swamp, when a rabbit popped up twenty feet away. He had broken his freeze behind a clump of dry grass, and he went skittering across the path. Almost without thinking, I took off the safety and threw the gun to my shoulder and fired.

65. What a shot! The rabbit gave one jump, about five feet in the air, then fell down and lay there kicking. I could hardly believe it. A running rabbit, going across the field—with a .22! Wait till I tell Dad, I thought.

66. "Did you see that, Billy?" I shouted.

67. Billy had seen, all right. Not even stopping to find out if I was going to fire again, he ran ahead of me up to the rabbit. When I got there he had the rabbit in his arms and he was cuddling it as if it were a puppy.

68. "You promised you wouldn't, Joe; you promised you wouldn't!" Billy was staring at me, his eyes angry.

69. "Aw, it's only a rabbit." I had to kid him out of this. "Mighty good eating too."

70. "Oh, no!" Billy said. "Oh, no!"

71. I took the rabbit from him.

72. "Come on," I said. "Come to my house and I'll show you how to skin it. The skin comes right off, just like a sweater. Then Mom'll fix it for supper and you can stay. . . ."

73. "No, no, no!" Before I knew it, Billy was off, half running up the hill through the cedars.

74. I took the rabbit home and skinned it, but it wasn't the fun it should have been. Mom fixed it for supper—I knew she would, since it was my birthday. I wanted to surprise Dad, and tell him about my lucky shot after Mom brought the rabbit to the table. But that didn't turn out so well, either. Dad lifted the covered dish (Mom had made it into a fricassee) and poked at the cut-up pieces with a serving spoon. Then he said, looking at me with a straight face, "Umm, it's been a long time since I've tasted stewed cat."

75. It was kind of hard to eat any after that. Dad and his corny jokes! What a birthday!

76. Sunday, after dinner, I was fooling around with the rabbit skin, scraping it and putting it on a frame to dry, when I saw Billy coming up the road. I covered the skin with an old sack to get it out of sight.

77. "Hi, Joe!" Billy called. He wasn't still angry about my shooting the rabbit. "See what I got for Wullie."

78. He held out a big brown bag so I could see inside. It was full of table scraps. There was a slice of ham, hardly eaten. Mom would never have thrown out a piece of meat like that.

79. "And now look at this," Billy said, and fished in his jacket pocket, bringing out a tube and a small bottle. "Penicillin and vitamins. We'll fix old Wullie up, all right."

80. Billy was like to bust with excitement. "Come on!" Then, kind of doubtful, "You want to come, don't you?"

81. "Sure," I said. "Of course I want to come. Just let me tell Mom we're going."

82. I went into the house and up to my room to get the gun. I picked it up. Sure was a sweet little rifle. But we probably wouldn't have any time for the quarry today. Besides, cartridges were kind of expensive, with two of us shooting.

83. It was only about a half-hour's walk to Rafe Jones's place the way I took Billy that day. "How come you know so much about dogs?" I said. "Thought you never had one."

84. "Never did. Dad says no dog till we settle somewhere."

85. "You could take him with you when you move."

86. "Oh, no, it wouldn't be fair: keeping him cooped up all the time. But if I lived where you do, Joe . . . Boy, oh, boy!"

87. "Yeah," I said. "I been thinking about a dog." I had been going to say a rabbit dog, but changed it.

88. We came out on the shoulder of the hill and looked down on the hollow where Rafe's place was. The dog—Wullie—was lying down, kind of listless. The beat-up old truck was sitting there under the maple tree.

89. "Aw, that's too bad," I said, but I felt kind of relieved. "Rafe's there." I turned back.

90. "Where you going?"

91. "We can't see Wullie when Rafe's there. You heard him."

92. "Sure I heard." Billy was scornful. "And I'm going to ask his permission to feed his dog. You don't have to come."

93. "Oh, I'll come," I said, but I wasn't too happy about it.

94. I followed Billy into the hollow. Wullie saw us coming and started to charge at us the way he had the day before. Billy didn't go to Wullie. Instead, he marched straight up to the front door, knocked, and knocked again. Then he peered through the dirty glass pane.

95. "He's there all right," Billy said. "Asleep."

96. "Drunk."

97. "All right, come on. He won't bother us any."

98. We went back toward the chicken house and

Wullie charged, snarling. Billy did just what he'd done the day before. He stood perfectly still until Wullie got tired, then held out the back of his hand for Wullie to sniff. It didn't take long for Billy to get to the overturned bucket. I guess Wullie smelled the food. Before Billy gave it to him he poured on some of the vitamin stuff from the little bottle, then spread the meat on the bag. Wullie wolfed the food in about two seconds. All the while Billy kept talking to him in that wheedling sing-song.

99. When Wullie had licked the paper clean he came to Billy, sniffing for more. Billy had the tube of penicillin ready. He squeezed two inches of it on his fingers. He let his hand slide up to the sore place under the collar.

100. Wullie's head snapped around with a snarl. Billy held still and didn't take his hand away, and Wullie didn't bite. Then Billy's fingers found the sore place again and began to rub in the ointment. All the while, Billy kept on talking. Wullie stood with his head down, letting Billy take care of him. His old sickle tail hung straight down between his legs. That dog couldn't even wag his tail.

101. "Now ain't that a real purty pitcher!" At the sound of Rafe's voice, Wullie snarled at Billy—but didn't bite. Rafe was at the end of the runway, weaving a little until he put his hand against the old maple. Neither of us had seen him.

102. "Thought I told you kids to stay off'n my place," Rafe said. "You deaf, or just plain ornery?"

103. Billy stood up, slowly, to face him. "I tried to ask your permission, sir."

104. Rafe blinked at the "sir," but Billy wasn't trying to be funny. "Well you ain't got it, fancy boy," Rafe said. "I don't want that dog gentled. He's there for just one reason: to keep out chicken thieves and little sneaks."

105. Billy, very slowly, left the run.

106. "I was only trying to help him," Billy said.

107. I could see the next thought flash into Rafe's mind.

108. "That's a valuable dog," Rafe said. "I'll sell him to you for . . . ten bucks."

109. "I don't have any place to keep a dog," Billy said.

110. Rafe's sly smile was wiped off his face. He took a step toward Billy and raised an arm. "Then git, the both of you, and don't come back!"

111. Rafe turned and walked disgustedly to Wullie, who was standing, head down, hackles bristling. Rafe lifted a booted foot and kicked Wullie in the belly. Wullie ki-yied.

112. Rafe swung his arm toward us. "Get'em, you mutt!"

113. Wullie charged until the chain bit into his neck. We heard his snarls even after we were out of sight.

114. At school on Monday Billy told me that his father had got the word last night: they had to move again. "Gee, that's too bad, Billy," I said. "I sure hate to see you go. I'll miss you a lot."

115. "I like it here. You sure are lucky, Joe."

116. "Oh, I don't know." Billy was the lucky one, I thought.

117. "We have to leave as soon as we can," Billy said. "Say—you want to come with me after school? I want to say goodbye to old Wullie."

118. "Gee, Billy, I don't know. Do you think . . ."

119. "Why don't you bring your gun along? We can stop in the quarry afterwards. I'll buy the cartridges."

120. "You don't have to buy'em." Billy always seemed to have money. I told you he was the lucky one.

121. "I want to buy'em," said Billy. "And I think I'll get old Wullie some real grub, too."

122. "Okay, Billy," I said. It'd be fun at the quarry.

123. As soon as school was out we stopped at the hardware store for cartridges, and Billy stopped off for meat. He bought a big knuckle bone for twenty-five cents, and then he got two pounds of ground round for a dollar seventy-five. That was better than we ate at home. Mom always bought chuck for hamburger. I stopped in at the house to pick up the gun, and we were off. It felt good to walk with a gun under my arm.

124. When we got to Rafe's place, I was relieved to see his truck wasn't in the yard. Old Wullie started the same old snarling charge, but he didn't keep it up more than about ten seconds when Billy held out the back of his hand. I stood around outside the runway, keeping my eyes and ears open for Rafe's truck. I sure didn't want to tangle with him again.

125 Billy went right in and sat on the bucket and gave Wullie the meat. Wullie just seemed to inhale it. Then Billy gave him the knuckle bone and Wullie lay down and held it between his big forepaws, and worked on it with his yellow teeth. All the time Billy was talking to him in that way he had.

126. Then Billy got up and came to where I was standing.

127. "Let me have your gun a minute," he said, and took it from my hand. He reached into his pocket for the new box of cartridges and loaded the gun.

128. He carried the gun with him and went back to sit on the bucket. Wullie rolled his eyes and made a noise deep in his throat, the way a dog does when he's enjoying a bone.

129. Then Billy put the muzzle of the gun behind Wullie's ear and pulled the trigger. With the shot, Wullie sighed and rolled on his side. The sickle tail flipped twice in the dust.

130. That's the only time we ever saw it wag.

131. Then Billy was sitting in the dirt holding Wullie's head in his lap, with a trickle of blood spreading on his pants. And then Billy leaned down and kissed the dirty old head.

132. Pretty soon he got up, picked up the gun and brought it to me. He reached into his inside pocket and took out a new ten-dollar bill. He looked around, kind of blindly, for a stone. He went back to Wullie and put the ten-dollar bill on his ribs, and weighted it carefully with the stone.

133. As we started off, we heard the rattle and groan of Rafe's truck coming up the road, but we never looked back.

Guide to Analysis

A. SCENES:

1. There are fourteen scenes, four narrative sections (the first one relatively long, from paragraph 1 through paragraph 11), and five short transitions. Bracket and label each of these scenes, and narrative and transitional passages.

2. Analyze the structural content of the first narrative section. Why is the second narrative section (paragraphs 23 through 26) necessary?

3. Find in Scenes Two, Four, Eleven, and Twelve the specific preparations for the end result.

4. Paragraphs 119 through 121 are necessary as con-sequential action in preparation for the result. Do they "give away" the end too early for you? Why? Why not? In answering these questions, stay within the report.

5. In Scene Three, paragraph 40, a drunken Rafe throws a bottle and hits Wullie neatly in the head. Do you believe this? Why? Why not? Confine your reasoning to the report.

6. Analyze, as examples of detail, the sensory report in Scenes One, Two, and Eleven.

B. STRUCTURE:

1. This is Billy's story; he decides; his decisions bring about the Middle and the End. Joe is the observing reporter. He is subjective, reporting his own inside-the-skin reactions as well as what he sees. But he reports Billy objectively. We do not get inside Billy's skin. Thus Billy's story is reported from the third person objective point of view, and there are no violations. Joe is an interesting character, and the events impinge on him and affect him (as we shall see in later questions), but it is Billy's story we must analyze for structure (fill in the outline):

I. The causative situation:

II. The deciding character:

a. his governing characteristic:

b. his problem:

    his first solution:

      its intensification:

    his second solution:

      its intensifications (there are at least three):

    his third solution:

III. The result:

a. for Billy:

b. for Joe:

2. Identify the three parts of the story.

3. Are paragraphs 77 and 80 in Scene Eight violations of the objective point of view?

4. We never see Billy fire the rifle till the last scene, and we do not see Joe teach Billy how to shoot as he had promised. Why? Has Mr. White slipped up in his con-sequential action report? Are you satisfied with this handling?

5. Study Billy's lines in the dialogue of Scene Six, paragraphs 68 through 73. Do they make Billy seem effeminate? Why? Why not? Be specific.

6. Is the result inevitable? Support your judgment fully.

7. What are the advantages of the point of view used in this story? What are some disadvantages?

C. CHARACTER:

1. Indicate throughout the story those sentences tagging Billy's governing characteristic. What else do we know about his character?

2. What does paragraph 16 indicate about Joe? What do paragraphs 75 and 76 indicate about Joe's character?

3. Which boy has more courage?

4. Why should the narrator (Joe) be made less admirable than the deciding actor (Billy)?

D. STORY IDEA:

1. State the story idea in a sentence and support your judgment with specific reference to the scenes.

THROUGH THE TUNNEL
by Doris Lessing

"Through the Tunnel" by Doris Lessing appeared first in The New Yorker *in 1955. Miss Lessing was born in Persia, grew up in South Africa, and is now an English citizen, publishing in New York and London. Her stories possess a subtle insight and penetration, both qualities demonstrated in this story of the age-old human desire for physical test of stamina. Why do people do impossible things at incalculable risk? Men climb mountains, they say, "because the mountain is there."*

1. Going to the shore on the first morning of the holiday, the young English boy stopped at a turning of the path and looked down at a wild and rocky bay, and then over to the crowded beach he knew so well from other years. His mother walked on in front of him, carrying a bright striped bag in one hand. Her other arm, swinging loose, was very white in the sun.

2. The boy watched that white, naked arm, and turned his eyes, which had a frown behind them, toward the bay and back again to his mother. When she felt he was not with her, she swung around.

3. "Oh, there you are, Jerry!" she said. She looked impatient, then smiled. "Why, darling, would you rather not come with me? Would you rather—" she frowned, conscientiously worrying over what amusements he might secretly be longing for which she had been too busy to imagine.

4. He was very familiar with that anxious, apologetic smile. Contrition sent him running after her. And yet, as he ran, he looked back over his shoulder at the wild bay; and all morning, as he played on the safe beach, he was thinking of it.

5. Next morning when it was time for the routine of swimming and sunbathing, his mother said, "Are you tired of the usual beach, Jerry? Would you like to go somewhere else?"

6. "Oh, no!" he said quickly, smiling at her out of that unfailing impulse of contrition—a sort of chivalry. Yet, walking down the path with her, he blurted out, "I'd like to go and have a look at those rocks down there."

7. She gave the idea her attention. It was a wild-looking place, and there was no one there, but she said, "Of course, Jerry. When you've had enough, come to the big beach. Or just go straight back to the villa, if you like."

8. She walked away, that bare arm, now slightly reddened from yesterday's sun, swinging. And he almost ran after her again, feeling it unbearable that she should go by herself, but he did not.

9. She was thinking. Of course he's old enough to be safe without me. Have I been keeping him too close? He mustn't feel he ought to be with me. I must be careful.

10. He was an only child, eleven years old. She was a widow. She was determined to be neither possessive nor lacking in devotion. She went worrying off to her beach.

11. As for Jerry, once he saw that his mother had gained her beach, he began the steep descent to the bay. From where he was, high up among red-brown rocks, it was a scoop of moving bluish green fringed with white.

12. As he went lower, he saw that it spread among small promontories and inlets of rough, sharp rock, and the crisping, lapping surface showed stains of purple and darker blue. Finally, as he ran sliding and scraping down the last few yards, he saw an edge of white surf, and the shallow, luminous movement of water over white sand, and, beyond that, a solid, heavy blue.

13. He ran straight into the water and began swimming. He was a good swimmer. He went out fast over the gleaming sand, over a middle region where rocks lay like discolored monsters under the surface, and then he was in the real sea—a warm sea where irregular cold currents from the deep water shocked his limbs.

14. When he was so far out that he could look back not only on the little bay but past the promontory that was between it and the big beach, he floated on the buoyant surface and looked for his mother. There she was, a speck of yellow under an umbrella that looked like a slice of orange peel. He swam back to shore, relieved at being sure she was there, but all at once very lonely.

15. On the edge of a small cape that marked the side of the bay away from the promontory was a loose scatter of rocks. Above them, some boys were stripping off their clothes. They came running, naked, down to the rocks.

16. The English boy swam toward them, and kept his distance at a stone's throw. They were of that coast, all of them burned smooth dark brown, and speaking a language he did not understand. To be with them, of them, was a craving that filled his whole body. He swam a little closer; they turned and watched him with narrowed, alert dark eyes.

17. Then one smiled and waved. It was enough. In a minute, he had swum in and was on the rocks beside them, smiling with a desperate, nervous supplication. They shouted cheerful greetings at him, and then, as he preserved his nervous, uncomprehending smile, they understood that he was a foreigner strayed from his own beach, and they proceeded to forget him. But he was happy. He was with them.

18. They began diving again and again from a high point into a well of blue sea between rough, pointed rocks. After they had dived and come up, they swam around, hauled themselves up, and waited their turn to dive again.

19. They were big boys—men to Jerry. He dived, and they watched him and when he swam around to take his place, they made way for him. He felt he was accepted, and he dived again, carefully, proud of himself.

20. Soon the biggest of the boys poised himself, shot down into the water, and did not come up. The others stood about watching. Jerry, after waiting for the sleek

brown head to appear, let out a yell of warning; they looked at him idly and turned their eyes back toward the water.

21. After a long time, the boy came up on the other side of a big dark rock, letting the air out of his lungs in a sputtering gasp and a shout of triumph. Immediately, the rest of them dived in. One moment, the morning seemed full of chattering boys; the next, the air and the surface of the water were empty. But through the heavy blue, dark shapes could be seen moving and groping.

22. Jerry dived, shot past the school of underwater swimmers, saw a black wall of rock looming at him, touched it, and bobbed up at once to the surface, where the wall was a low barrier he could see across. There was no one visible; under him, in the water, the dim shapes of the swimmers had disappeared. Then one, and then another of the boys came up on the far side of the barrier of rock, and he understood that they had swum through some gap or hole in it. He plunged down again.

23. He could see nothing through the stinging salt water but the blank rock. When he came up, the boys were all on the diving rock, preparing to attempt the feat again. And now, in a panic of failure, he yelled up, in English, "Look at me! Look!" and he began splashing and kicking in the water like a foolish dog.

24. They looked down gravely, frowning. He knew the frown. At moments of failure, when he clowned to claim his mother's attention, it was with just this grave embarrassed inspection that she rewarded him.

25. Through his hot shame, feeling the pleading grin on his face like a scar that he could never remove, he looked up at the group of big brown boys on the rock and shouted "Bonjour! Merci! Au revoir! Monsieur, monsieur!" while he hooked his fingers round his ears and waggled them.

26. Water surged into his mouth; he choked, sank, came up. The rock, lately weighted with the boys, seemed to rear up out of the water as their weight was removed. They were flying down past him, now, into the water; the air was full of falling bodies. Then the

rock was empty in the hot sunlight. He counted, one, two, three. . . .

27. At fifty, he was terrified. They must all be drowning beneath him, in the watery caves of the rock! At a hundred, he stared around him at the empty hillside, wondering if he should yell for help.

28. He counted faster, faster, to hurry them up, to bring them to the surface quickly, to drown them quickly—anything rather than the terror of counting on and on into the blue emptiness of the morning. And then, at a hundred and sixty, the water beyond the rock was full of boys blowing like brown whales. They swam back to the shore without a look at him.

29. He climbed back to the diving rock and sat down, feeling the hot roughness of it under his thighs. The boys were gathering up their bits of clothing and running off along the shore to another promontory.

30. They were leaving to get away from him. He cried openly, fists in his eyes. There was no one to see him, and he cried himself out.

31. It seemed to him that a long time had passed and he swam out to where he could see his mother. Yes, she was still there, a yellow spot under an orange umbrella. He swam back to the big rock, climbed up, and dived into the blue pool among the fanged and angry boulders. Down he went, until he touched the wall of rock again. But the salt was so painful in his eyes that he could not see.

32. He came to the surface, swam to shore and went back to the villa to wait for his mother. Soon she walked slowly up the path, swinging her striped bag, the flushed, naked arm dangling beside her. "I want some swimming goggles," he panted, defiant and beseeching.

33. She gave him a patient, inquisitive look as she said casually, "Well, of course, darling."

34. But now, now now! He must have them this minute, and no other time. He nagged and pestered until she went with him to a shop. As soon as she had bought the goggles, he grabbed them from her hand as if she were going to claim them for herself, and was off, running down the steep path to the bay.

35. Jerry swam out to the big barrier rock, adjusted the goggles, and dived. The impact of the water broke the rubber-enclosed vacuum, and the goggles came loose.

36. He understood that he must swim down to the base of the rock from the surface of the water. He fixed the goggles tight and firm, filled his lungs, and floated, face down on the water.

37. Now he could see. It was as if he had eyes of a different kind—fish-eyes that showed everything clear and delicate and wavering in the bright water.

38. Under him, six or seven feet down, was a floor of perfectly clean, shining white sand, rippled firm and hard by the tides. Two grayish shapes steered there, like long, rounded pieces of wood or slate.

39. They were fish. He saw them nose toward each other, poise motionless, make a dart forward, swerve off, and come around again. It was like a water dance.

40. A few inches above them, the water sparkled as if sequins were dropping through it. Fish again—myriads of minute fish, the length of his fingernail, were drifting through the water, and in a moment he could feel the innumerable tiny touches of them, against his limbs. It was like swimming in flaked silver.

41. The great rock the big boys had swum through rose sheer out of the white sand, black, tufted lightly with greenish weed. He could see no gap in it. He swam down to its base.

42. Again and again he rose, took a big chestful of air, and went down. Again and again he groped over the surface of the rock, feeling it, almost hugging it in the desperate need to find the entrance.

43. And then, once, while he was clinging to the black wall, his knees came up and he shot his feet out forward and they met no obstacle. He had found the hole.

44. He gained the surface, clambered about the stones that littered the barrier rock until he found a big one, and with this in his arms, let himself down over the side of the rock. He dropped, with the weight, to the sandy floor.

45. Clinging tight to the anchor of the stone, he lay on his side and looked in under the dark shelf at the place where his feet had gone. He could see the hole.

46. It was an irregular, dark gap, but he could not see deep into it. He let go of his anchor, clung with his hands to the edges of the hole, and tried to push himself in.

47. He got his head in, found his shoulders jammed, moved them in sidewise, and was inside as far as his waist. He could see nothing ahead.

48. Something soft and clammy touched his mouth. He saw a dark frond moving against the grayish rock, and panic filled him. He thought of octopuses, or clinging weed.

49. He pushed himself out backward and caught a glimpse, as he retreated, of a harmless tentacle of seaweed drifting in the mouth of the tunnel. But it was enough.

50. He reached the sunlight, swam to shore, and lay on the diving rock. He looked down into the blue well of water. He knew he must find his way through that cave, or hole, or tunnel, and out the other side.

51. First, he thought, he must learn to control his breathing. He let himself down into the water with another big stone in his arms, so that he could lie effortlessly on the bottom.

52. One, two, three. He counted steadily. He could hear the movement of blood in his head. Fifty-one, fifty-two. . . .

53. His chest was hurting. He let go of the rock and went up into the air. He saw that the sun was low. He rushed to the villa and found his mother at her supper. She said only, "Did you enjoy yourself?" and he said, "Yes."

54. All night, the boy dreamed of the water-filled cave in the rock, and as soon as breakfast was over he went to the bay.

55. That night, his nose bled badly. For hours he had been underwater, learning to hold his breath, and now he felt weak and dizzy. His mother said, "I shouldn't overdo things, darling, if I were you."

56. That day and the next, Jerry exercised his lungs as if everything, the whole of his life, all that he would become, depended upon it. Again his nose bled at night, and his mother insisted on his coming with her the next day.

57. It was a torment to him to waste a day of his careful self-training, but he stayed with her on that other beach, which now seemed a place for small children, a place where his mother might lie safe in the sun. It was not his beach.

58. He did not ask for permission, on the following day, to go to his beach. He went, before his mother could consider the complicated rights and wrongs of the matter.

59. A day's rest, he discovered, had improved his count by ten. The big boys had made the passage while he counted a hundred and sixty. He had been counting fast, in his fright. Probably now, if he tried, he could get through that long tunnel, but he was not going to try yet.

60. A curious, most unchildlike persistence, a controlled impatience, made him wait. In the meantime, he lay underwater on the white sand, littered now by stones he had brought down from the upper air, and studied the entrance to the tunnel. He knew every jut and corner of it, as far as it was possible to see. It was as if he already felt its sharpness about his shoulders.

61. He sat by the clock in the villa, when his mother was not near, and checked his time. He was incredulous and then proud to find he could hold his breath without strain for two minutes. The words "two minutes," authorized by the clock, brought the adventure that was so necessary to him close.

62. In another four days, his mother said casually one morning, they must go home. On the day before they left, he would do it. He would do it if it killed him, he said defiantly to himself. But two days before they were to leave—a day of triumph when he increased his count by fifteen—his nose bled so badly that he turned dizzy and had to lie limply over the big rock like a bit of seaweed, watching the thick red blood

flow onto the rock and trickle slowly down to the sea. He was frightened.

63. Supposing he turned dizzy in the tunnel? Supposing he died there, trapped? Supposing—his head went around in the hot sun, and he almost gave up. He thought he would return to the house and lie down, and next summer, perhaps, when he had another year's growth in him—then he would go through the hole.

64. But even after he had made the decision, or thought he had, he found himself sitting up on the rock and looking down into the water, and he knew that now, this moment, when his nose had only just stopped bleeding, when his head was still sore and throbbing—this was the moment when he would try. If he did not do it now, he never would.

65. He was trembling with fear that he would not go, and he was trembling with horror at that long, long tunnel under the rock, under the sea. Even in the open sunlight, the barrier rock seemed very wide and very heavy; tons of rock pressed down on where he would go. If he died there, he would lie until one day—perhaps not before next year—those big boys would swim into it and find it blocked.

66. He put on his goggles, fitted them tight, tested the vacuum. His hands were shaking. Then he chose the biggest stone he could carry and slipped over the edge of the rock until half of him was in the cool, enclosing water and half in the hot sun.

67. He looked up once at the empty sky, filled his lungs once, twice, and then sank fast to the bottom with the stone. He let it go and began to count. He took the edges of the hole in his hands and drew himself into it, wriggling his shoulders in sidewise as he remembered he must.

68. Soon he was clear inside. He was in a small rock-bound hole filled with yellowish-gray water. The water was pushing him up against the roof. The roof was sharp and pained his back. He pulled himself along with his hands—fast, fast—and used his legs as levers.

69. His head knocked against something; a sharp pain dizzied him. Fifty, fifty-one, fifty-two . . . . He

was without light, and the water seemed to press upon him with the weight of rock. Seventy-one, seventy-two. . . . There was no strain on his lungs. He felt like an inflated balloon, his lungs were so light and easy, but his head was pulsing.

70. He was being continually pressed against the sharp roof, which felt slimy as well as sharp. Again he thought of octopuses, and wondered if the tunnel might be filled with weed that could tangle him. He gave himself a panicky, convulsive kick forward, ducked his head, and swam.

71. His feet and hands moved freely, as if in open water. The hole must have widened out. He thought he must be swimming fast, and he was frightened of banging his head if the tunnel narrowed.

72. A hundred, a hundred and one. . . . The water paled. Victory filled him. His lungs were beginning to hurt. A few more strokes and he would be out. He was counting wildly; he said a hundred and fifteen, and then, a long time later, a hundred and fifteen again. The water was a clear jewel-green all around him. Then he saw, above his head, a crack running up through the rock. Sunlight was falling through it, showing the clean dark rock of the tunnel, a single mussel shell, and darkness ahead.

73. He was at the end of what he could do. He looked up at the crack as·if it were filled with air and not water, as if he could put his mouth to it to draw in air. A hundred and fifteen, he heard himself say inside his head—but he had said that long ago.

74. He must go on into the blackness ahead, or he would drown. His head was swelling, his lungs cracking. A hundred and fifteen, a hundred and fifteen pounded through his head, and he feebly clutched at rocks in the dark, pulling himself forward, leaving the brief space of sunlit water behind.

75. He felt he was dying. He was no longer quite conscious. He struggled on in the darkness between lapses into unconsciousness. An immense, swelling pain filled his head, and then the darkness cracked with an explosion of green light. His hands, groping for-

ward, met nothing, and his feet, kicking back, propelled him out into the open sea.

76. He drifted to the surface, his face turned up to the air. He was gasping like a fish. He felt he would sink now and drown; he could not swim the few feet back to the rock. Then he was clutching it and pulling himself up onto it.

77. He lay face down, gasping. He could see nothing but a red-veined, clotted dark. His eyes must have burst, he thought; they were full of blood. He tore off his goggles and a gout of blood went into the sea. His nose was bleeding, and the blood had filled the goggles.

78. He scooped up handfuls of water from the cool, salty sea, to splash on his face, and did not know whether it was blood or salt water he tasted. After a time, his heart quieted, his eyes cleared, and he sat up.

79. He could see the local boys diving and playing half a mile away. He did not want them. He wanted nothing but to get back home and lie down.

80. In a short while, Jerry swam to shore and climbed slowly up the path to the villa. He flung himself on his bed and slept, waking at the sound of feet on the path outside. His mother was coming back. He rushed to the bathroom, thinking she must not see his face with bloodstains, or tearstains, on it. He came out of the bathroom and met her as she walled into the villa.

81. "Have a nice morning?" she asked, laying her hand on his warm brown shoulder a moment.

82. "Oh, yes, thank you," he said.

83. "You look a bit pale." And then, sharp and anxious, "How did you bang your head?"

84. "Oh, just banged it," he told her.

85. She looked at him closely. He was strained. His eyes were glazed-looking. She was worried. And then she said to herself, "Oh, don't fuss! Nothing can happen. He can swim like a fish."

86. They sat down to lunch together.

87. "Mummy," he said. "I can stay under water for two minutes—three minutes, at least." It came bursting out of him.

88. "Can you, darling?" she said. "Well, I shouldn't

overdo it. I don't think you ought to swim any more today."

89. She was ready for a battle of wills, but he gave in at once. It was no longer of the least importance to go to the bay.

Guide to Analysis

A. SCENES:

1. This story is presented in sixteen scenes, with three sections of narrative and two passages of transition. Bracket the scenes exactly and indicate the other passages. Remember, a scene occurs in a particular time and place and with a particular character.

2. Compare the sensory development of scene in this story with that in "Bush Boy, Poor Boy" or "Sled." What effect does scene development have on story interest? On story idea? On the story significance?

3. Scene Thirteen is progressive, that is, we move through the tunnel so that "place" seems to change. What holds the scene in one place? Why is this scene not a transition from one end of the tunnel to the other? What is the essential difference between the narrative section following Scene Eleven and the progression in Scene Thirteen?

4. In Scene Thirteen, underline the words dealing with light.

5. Would you say that "Through the Tunnel" is well scened? Explain.

B. STRUCTURE:

1. List the fragments which present the panoramic view. Is this part of structure sufficiently well presented for you? Why?

2. Place the story on this structural outline and indicate the sentences which first present each part of structure.

   I. The causative situation:

   II. The deciding character:

      a. his governing characteristic:

b. his problem:

>his first solution decided:
>
>>the first interference:
>
>his second solution decided:
>
>>the second interference:
>
>his third solution decided:

III. The result:

3. Is the result inevitable? Justify your judgment with specific sentences.

4. Indicate the end of the Beginning and the end of the Middle.

5. Describe the point of view here. Do you find violations? Are these violations justified by the effect produced? What would be lost to the story from a strict adherence to Jerry's point of view? What would have been gained?

6. Count the number of tags of Jerry's governing characteristic; of the mother-son relationship.

7. Jerry's central problem is complicated by his relationship to his mother and to the boys. How does this enrich the story significance? Such complication could have been easily avoided. Would you have done so? Defend your judgment.

8. Do you think the decision in paragraph 64, coming after the tentative decision in the preceding two paragraphs, is realistic and believable? Defend your judgment specifically.

9. What insights into Jerry do you get in the long narrative passage between paragraphs 49 and 62? Why are these insights necessary? Justify the use of narrative here in place of scene.

C. DIALOGUE:

1. In this story the dialogue is limited to only the first two scenes and the last scene, with fragments in the narrative sections. There are at least three good reasons. Can you see these reasons?

2. What effect on the story comes from the absence of dialogue in all but three scenes?

3. How does the dialogue illuminate the mother's character? What can you learn of her from what she says?

D. THE STORY IDEA:

1. State the idea of this story in one sentence.

2. Where, specifically, do you find the idea presented in the scenes and narrative sections? Where implied by action? By dialogue?

3. Why did Jerry cry in Scene Nine? Do you believe this? Why?

4. Why was it "no longer of the least importance" to Jerry "to go to the bay"? Have you been sufficiently prepared for this ending? Where?

SLED

by Thomas E. Adams

Stories are made of actual life processes rearranged to fit the requirements of an artistic discipline. "Sled" perfectly illustrates this use of the commonplace. It is a story which, partly by brilliant report of sensory scene, reports the episode of a boy, whose pride has been injured by his sister and who "gets back" at her by letting her ride a broken sled and by blaming her for the break. How simple? But how movingly true. The scene reports here will pay you for careful analysis.

"Sled" appeared first in Sewanee Review *in 1961 and won the O'Henry Award in 1962, four years after Adams had graduated from LaSalle College, Philadelphia, Pennsylvania.*

1. All the adventure of the night and snow lay before him: if only he could get out of the house.

2. "You can't go out," his mother said, "until you learn how to act like a gentleman. Now apologize to your sister."

3. He stared across the table at his sister.

4. "Go on," his mother said.

5. His sister was watching her plate. He could detect the trace of a smile at the corners of her mouth.

6. "I won't! She's laughing at me!" He saw the smile grow more pronounced. "Besides, she is a liar!"

7. His sister did not even bother to look up, and he felt from looking at her that he had said exactly what she had wanted him to say. He grew irritated at his stupidity.

8. "That settles it," his mother said calmly, without turning from the stove. "No outs for you."

9. He stared at his hands, his mind in a panic. He could feel the smile on his sister's face. His hand fumbled with the fork on his plate. "No," he said meekly, prodding a piece of meat with the fork. "I'll apologize."

10. His sister looked up at him innocently.

11. "Well?" said his mother. "Go on."

12. He took a deep breath. "I'm . . ." He met his sister's gaze. "I'm sorry!" But it came out too loudly, he knew.

13. "He is not," his sister said.

14. He clenched his teeth and pinched his legs with his fingers. "I am too," he said. It sounded good, he knew; and it was half over. He had control now, and he relaxed a bit and even said further: "I'm sorry I called you a liar."

15. "That's better," his mother said. "You two should love each other. Not always be fighting."

16. He paused strategically for a long moment.

17. "Can I go out now?"

18. "Yes," his mother said.

19. He rose from the table glaring at his sister with a broad grin, calling her a liar with his eyes.

20. His hand plucked his jacket from the couch and swirled it around his back. The buttons refused to fit through the holes, so he let them go in despair. He sat down just long enough to pull on his shiny black rubbers. Finally he put on his gloves. Then with four proud strides he arrived at the door and reached for the knob.

21. "Put your hat on," his mother said without looking at him.

22. His face toward the door, screwed and tightened with disgust. "Aw, Ma."

23. "Put it on."

24. "Aw, Ma, it's not that cold."

25. "Put it on."

26. "Honest, Ma, it's not that cold out."

27. "Are you going to put your hat on, or are you going to stay and help with the dishes?"

28. He sighed. "All right," he said. "I'll put it on."

29. The door to the kitchen closed on his back and he was alone in the cold gloom of the shed. Pale light streamed through the frosted window and fell against the wall where the sled stood. The dark cold room was silent, and he was free. He moved into the shaft of light and stopped, when from the kitchen he heard the muffled murmur of his mother's voice, as if she were far away. He listened. The murmuring hushed and he was alone again.

30. The sled. It was leaning against the wall, its varnished wood glistening in the moonlight. He moved closer to it and saw his shadow block the light, and he heard the cold cracking of the loose linoleum beneath his feet.

31. He picked it up. He felt the smooth wood slippery in his gloved hands. The thin steel runners shone blue in the light, as he moved one finger along the polished surface to erase any dust. He shifted the sled in his hands and stood getting the feel of its weight the way he had seen his brother hold a rifle. He gripped the sled tightly, aware of the strength in his arms; and he felt proud to be strong and alone and far away with the sled in the dark cold silent room.

32. The sled was small and light. But strong. And when he ran with it, he ran very quickly, quicker than anyone, because it was very light and small and not bulky like other sleds. And when he ran with it, he carried it as if it were part of him, as if he carried nothing in his arms. He set the rear end on the floor, now, and let the sled lean against him, his hands on the steering bar. He pushed down on the bar and the thin runners curved gracefully because they were made of shiny blue flexible steel; and with them he could turn sharply in the snow, sharper than anyone. It was the best sled. It was his.

33. He felt a slight chill in the cold room, and in the moonlight he saw his breath in vapor rising like cigarette smoke before his eyes. His body shivered with excitement as he moved hurriedly but noiselessly to the door. He flung it open; and the snow blue and sparkling, and the shadows deep and mysterious, the air silent and cold; all awaited him.

34. "Joey!" From the kitchen came his mother's voice. He turned toward the kitchen door and refused to answer.

35. "Joseph!"

36. "What!" His tone was arrogant, and a chill of fear rushed through his mind.

37. There was a long awful silence.

38. "Don't you forget to be home by seven o'clock." She hadn't noticed, and his fear was gone.

39. "All right!" He answered, ashamed of his fear. He stepped across the threshold and closed the door. Then he removed the hat and dropped it in the snow beside the porch.

40. He plodded down the alley, thrilling in the cold white silence—the snow was thick. The gate creaked as he pushed it open, holding and guiding the sled through the portal. The street was white, and shiny were the icy tracks of automobiles in the lamplight above. While between him and the light the black branches of trees ticked softly, in the slight wind. In the gutters stood enormous heaps of snow, pale and dark in the shadows, stretching away from him like a string of mountains. He moved out of the shadows, between two piles of snow, and into the center of the street; where he stood for a moment gazing down the white road that gradually grew darker until it melted into the gloom at the far end.

41. Then he started to trot slowly down the street. Slowly, slowly gaining speed without losing balance. Faster he went now, watching the snow glide beneath his shiny black rubbers. Faster and faster, but stiffly, don't slip. Don't fall, don't fall: now! And his body plunged downward and the sled whacked in the quiet and the white close to his eyes was flying beneath him as he felt the thrill of gliding alone along a shadowy

street, with only the ski-sound of the sled in the packed snow. Then before his eyes the moving snow gradually slowed. And stopped. And he heard only the low sound of the wind and his breath.

42. Up again and start the trot. He moved to the beating sound of his feet along the ground. His breath came heavily and quickly, and matched the rhythm of his pumping legs, straining to carry the weight of his body without the balance of his arms. He reached a wild dangerous breakneck speed, and his leg muscles swelled and ached from the tension, and the fear of falling too early filled his mind; and down he let his body go. The white road rushed to meet him; he was off again, guiding the sled obliquely across the street toward a huge pile of snow near a driveway.

43. Squinting his eyes into the biting wind, he calculated when he would turn to avoid crashing. The pile, framed against the darkness of the sky, glistened white and shiny. It loomed larger and larger before him. He steered the sled sharply, bending the bar; and the snow flew as the sled churned sideways, and he heard suddenly a cold metallic snap. He and the sled went tumbling over in the hard wet snow. He rolled with it and the steering bar jarred his forehead. Then the dark sky and snow stopped turning, and all he felt was the cold air stinging the bump on his forehead.

44. The runner had snapped; the sled was broken. He stared at the shiny smooth runner and touched the jagged edge with his fingers. He sat in the middle of the driveway, the sled cradled in his lap, running his fingers up and down the thin runner until he came to the jagged edge where it had broken.

45. With his fingers he took the two broken edges and fitted them back into place. They stuck together with only a thin crooked line to indicate the split. But it was like putting a broken cup together. He stared at it, and wished it would be all right and felt like crying.

46. He got up and walked slowly back down to the street to his house. He sat down between the back bumper of a parked car and a pile of snow. Cradling the sled across his legs, he put the two edges together again and stared at them. He felt a thickness in his

throat, and he swallowed hard to remove it, but it did not go away.

47. He leaned back, resting his head against the snowpile. Through his wet eyelids he saw the lamplight shimmering brightly against the sky. He closed his eyes and saw again the shiny graceful curve of the runner. But it was broken now. He had bent it too far; too far. With his hand he rubbed his neck, then his eyes, then his neck again. He felt the snow coming wet through his pants. As he shifted to a new position, he heard the creaking of a gate. He turned toward the sound.

48. His sister was walking away from his house. He watched her move slowly across the street and into the grocery store. Through the plate-glass window he saw her talking with the storekeeper. He stared down at the runner. With his gloves off, he ran his fingers along the cold smooth surface and felt the thin breakline. He got up, brushed the snow off the seat of his pants, and walked to the gate to wait for his sister.

49. He saw her take a package from the man and come out of the store. She walked carefully on the smooth white, her figure dark in its own shadow as she passed beneath the streetlight, the package in her arm. When she reached the curb on his side, he rested his arms on the nose of the sled and exhaled a deep breath nervously. He pretended to be staring in the opposite direction.

50. When he heard her feet crunching softly in the snow, he turned: "Hi," he said.

51. "Hi," she said and she paused for a moment. "Good sledding?"

52. "Uh-huh," he said. "Just right. Snow's packed nice and hard. Hardly any slush at all." He paused. "I'm just resting a bit now."

53. She nodded. "I just went for some milk."

54. His fingers moved slowly down the runner and touched the joined edges.

55. "Well . . ." she said, about to leave.

56. His fingers trembled slightly, and he felt his heart begin to beat rapidly: "Do you want to take a flop?" In the still night air he heard with surprise the calm sound of his voice.

57. Her face came suddenly alive. "Can I? I mean, will you let me? Really?"

58. "Sure," he said. "Go ahead." And he handed her the sled very carefully. She gave him the package.

59. He put the bag under his arm and watched her move out of the shadows of the trees and into the light. She started to trot slowly, awkwardly, bearing the sled. She passed directly beneath the light and then she slipped and slowed to regain her balance. The sled looked large and heavy in her arms, and seeing her awkwardness, he realized, she would be hurt badly in the fall. She was moving away again, out of the reach of the streetlight, and into the gray haze farther down the road.

60. He moved to the curb, holding the bag tightly under his arm, hearing his heart pounding in his ears. He wanted to stop her, and he opened his mouth as if to call her; but no sound came. It was too late: her dark figure was already starting the fall, putting the sled beneath her. Whack! And her head dipped with the front end jutting the ground, and the back of the sled and her legs rose like a seesaw and down they came with another muffled sound. The street was quiet, except for a low whimper that filled his ears.

61. He saw her figure rise slowly and move toward him. He walked out to meet her beneath the light. She held the sled loosely in one hand, the broken runner, dangling, reflecting light as she moved.

62. She sobbed and looking up he saw bright tears falling down her cheeks, and a thin line of blood trickling down her chin. In the corner of her mouth near the red swelling of her lip, a little bubble of spit shone with the blood in the light.

63. He felt that he should say something but he did not speak.

64. "I'm . . . I'm sorry," she said and the bubble broke. "I'm sorry I . . . your sled." She looked down at the sled. "It'll never be the same."

65. "It'll be all right," he said. He felt that he ought to do something but he did not move. "I can get it soldered. Don't worry about it." But he saw from her

expression that she thought he was only trying to make her feel better.

66. "No," she said, shaking her head emphatically. "No, it won't! It'll always have that weak spot now." She began to cry very hard. "I'm sorry."

67. He made an awkward gesture of forgiveness with his hand. "Don't cry," he said.

68. She kept crying.

69. "It wasn't your fault," he said.

70. "Yes, it was," she said. "Oh, yes, it was."

71. "No!" he said. "No, it wasn't!" But she didn't seem to hear him, and he felt his words were useless. He sighed wearily with defeat, not knowing what to say next. He saw her glance up at him as if to see whether he were still watching her, then she quickly lowered her gaze and said with despair and anguish: "Oh . . . girls are so stupid!"

72. There was no sound. She was no longer crying. She was looking at the ground: waiting. His ears heard nothing; they felt only the cold silent air.

73. "No, they aren't," he said half-heartedly. And he heard her breathing again. He felt he had been forced to say that. In her shining eyes he saw an expression he did not understand. He wished she would go to the house. But seeing the tears on her cheeks and the blood on her chin, he immediately regretted the thought.

74. She wiped her chin with her sleeve, and he winced, feeling rough cloth on an open cut. "Don't do that." His hand moved to his back pocket. "Use my handkerchief."

75. She waited.

76. The pocket was empty. "I haven't got one," he said.

77. Staring directly at him, she patted gingerly the swollen part of her lip with the tips of her fingers.

78. He moved closer to her. "Let me see," he said. With his hands he grasped her head and tilted it so that the light fell directly on the cut.

79. "It's not too bad," she said calmly. And as she said it she looked straight into his eyes, and he felt she

was perfectly at ease; while standing that close to her, he felt clumsy and out of place.

80. In his hands her head was small and fragile, and her hair was soft and warm; he felt the rapid pulsing of the vein in her temple; his ears grew hot with shame.

81. "Maybe I better go inside and wash it off?" she asked.

82. With his finger he wiped the blood from her chin. "Yes," he said, feeling relieved. "You go inside and wash it off." He took the sled and gave her the package.

83. He stared at the ground as they walked to the gate in silence. When they reached the curb he became aware that she was watching him.

84. "You've got a nasty bump on your forehead," she said.

85. "Yes," he said. "I fell."

86. "Let me put some snow on it," she said, reaching to the ground.

87. He caught her wrist and held it gently. "No," he said.

88. He saw her about to object: "It's all right. You go inside and take care of your lip." He said it softly but with his grip and his eyes he told her more firmly.

89. "All right," she said after a moment, and he released his hold. "But don't forget to put your hat on."

90. He stared at her.

91. "I mean, before you go back in the house."

92. They both smiled.

93. "Thanks for reminding me," he said, and he dropped the sled in the snow and hurried to hold the gate open for her.

94. She hesitated, then smiled proudly as he beckoned her into the alley.

95. He watched her walk away from him down the dark alley in the gray snow. Her small figure swayed awkwardly as she stepped carefully in the deep snow, so as not to get her feet too wet. Her head was bowed and her shoulders hunched and he humbly felt her weakness. And he felt her cold. And he felt the snow running cold down her boots around her ankles. And though she wasn't crying now, he could still hear her

low sobbing, and he saw her shining eyes and the tears falling and she trying to stop them and they fell even faster. And he wished he had never gone sledding. He wished that he had never even come out of the house tonight.

96. The back door closed. He turned and moved about nervously kicking at the ground. At the edge of the curb he dug his hands deep into the cold wet snow. He came up with a handful and absently began shaping and smoothing it. He stopped abruptly and dropped it at his feet.

97. He did not hear it fall. He was looking up at the dark sky but he did not see it. He put his cold hands in his back pockets but he did not feel them. He was wishing that he were some time a long time away from now and somewhere a long way away from here.

98. In the corner of his eye something suddenly dimmed. Across the street in the grocery store the light was out: it was seven o'clock.

Guide to Analysis

A. SCENES:

1. Bracket and number the scenes and transitions. I count ten scenes and four short transitions. Do you agree? Though you remember that a scene exists in a particular time and place, you must observe that the place in Scene Three is *the street*. And Scenes Four and Five take place on the sled, a different place from the street. Thus, Scene One runs from paragraph 1 through paragraph 28; Scene Two runs from paragraph 29 through the third sentence in paragraph 39; Scene Three runs from the third sentence in paragraph 40 through paragraph 40; and the Fourth Scene runs through paragraph 41. Complete the identification of scenes and transitions.

2. The first scene is a good, hard-working scene. List all the structural information given to us in this one scene.

3. Why does Adams report Scene Two in such a wealth of sensory detail?

4. All but the first scene are reported in the dark of night. How does Adams light his scenes? Underline all reports of light.

5. What is the effect of not using names in this story? We hear "Joey" only once.

6. Analyze completely the sensory elements of Scene Two and Scene Ten.

B. STRUCTURE:

1. Account fully for the absence of panoramic view in "Sled."

2. Fill in the following outline of structure. Observe that the story is duple: the major physical episodes of the sled, the sister, and the brother-sister relationship; and minor psychological story of the boy's mind and spirit.

   I. The causative situation:

  II. The deciding character:

      the minor characters:

     a. his governing characteristics:

      his minor characteristics:

     b. his problem:

      his minor problem:

        his first solution:

         first interference:

        his second solution:

         second interference (major and minor)

        his third solution:

         third interference:

        his fourth solution:

 III. The result:

     major:

     minor:

3. Describe the point of view used here. Observe the fact that it is never violated. How, specifically, does

this strict adherence to one point of view affect you?

4. Is the accident to the sled believable? What makes it so?

5. Are the results (minor and major) inevitable?

6. Oral communication breaks down between the two children. Are you prepared for this? Where, specifically?

7. Why are the last three paragraphs (final scene) necessary?

C. DIALOGUE:

1. Study the "he said" clauses in the dialogue. What words are used besides "said"? Underline the dialogue *tags* which contribute to an understanding of character; of structure.

2. Can you find any dialogue not used for structural purposes?

3. List the bits of dialogue that illuminate character.

4. What are the uses of the dialogue in paragraphs 21 through 28?

D. CHARACTER:

1. Make a complete analysis of Joey's character supporting yourself by lines from the scenes.

2. Make a prediction of Joey's adult character and support your judgment.

3. Which tells you most about Joey's character, the dialogue or the scene report?

HOW MR. HOGAN ROBBED A BANK
by John Steinbeck

This Steinbeck story, which first appeared in The Atlantic Monthly *in March 1956, is rich in lessons for the writer. You will want to examine for example, his choice of a long, beginning, narrative passage before the first scene report, in this case, a flashback coming before the causative situation has been introduced. How effective is this method? Does it have dangers or limitations? Note too, how Steinbeck uses consequent detail. No move is omitted; no act is related out of order; no unnecessary action is reported. Of additional interest is Steinbeck's manipulation of the third person subjective point of view, with subtle variations from that point of*

view. *How does he accomplish these variations? Why,
and to what effect?*

*The tone is lighthearted, a good-humored bantering
brand of satire. How does Steinback use understate-
ment to intensify humor? Does he manage to maintain
the tone throughout, without deflecting attention from
the plot?*

1. On the Saturday before Labor Day, 1955, at
9:04½ A.M., Mr. Hogan robbed a bank. He was forty-
two years old, married, and the father of a boy and
a girl, named John and Joan, twelve and thirteen re-
spectively. Mrs. Hogan's name was Joan and Mr. Hogan's was John, but since they called themselves Papa
and Mama that left their names free for the children,
who were considered very smart for their ages, each
having jumped a grade in school. The Hogans lived at
215 East Maple Street, in a brown-shingled house
with white trim—there are two. 215 is the one across
from the street light and it is the one with the big tree
in the yard, either oak or elm—the biggest tree in the
whole street, maybe in the whole town.

2. John and Joan were in bed at the time of the
robbery, for it was Saturday. At 9:10 A.M. Mrs. Hogan was making the cup of tea she always had. Mr.
Hogan went to work early. Mrs. Hogan drank her tea
slowly, scalding hot, and read her fortune in the tea
leaves. There was a cloud and a five-pointed star with
two short points in the bottom of the cup, but that was
at 9:12 and the robbery was all over by then.

3. The way Mr. Hogan went about robbing the bank
was very interesting. He gave it a great deal of thought
and had for a long time, but he did not discuss it with
anyone. He just read his newspaper and kept his own
counsel. But he worked it out to his own satisfaction
that people went to too much trouble robbing banks
and that got them in a mess. The simpler the better,
he always thought. People went in for too much hulla-
baloo and hanky-panky. If you didn't do that, if you
left hanky-panky out, robbing a bank would be a relatively sound venture—barring accidents, of course, of

an improbable kind, but then they could happen to a man crossing the street or anything. Since Mr. Hogan's method worked fine, it proved that his thinking was sound. He often considered writing a little booklet on his technique when the how-to rage was running so high. He figured out the first sentence, which went: "To successfully rob a bank, forget all about hanky-panky."

4. Mr. Hogan was not just a clerk at Fettucci's grocery store. He was more like the manager. Mr. Hogan was in charge, even hired and fired the boy who delivered groceries after school. He even put in orders with the salesmen, sometimes when Mr. Fettucci was right in the store, too, maybe talking to a customer. "You do it, John," he would say and he would nod at the customer, "John knows the ropes. Been with me—how long you been with me, John?"

5. "Sixteen years."

6. "Sixteen years. Knows the business as good as me. John, why he even banks the money."

7. And so he did. Whenever he had a moment, Mr. Hogan went into the storeroom on the alley, took off his apron, put on his necktie and coat, and went back through the store to the cash register. The checks and bills would be ready for him inside the bankbook with a rubber band around it. Then he went next door and stood at the teller's window and handed the checks and bankbook through to Mr. Cup and passed the time of day with him, too. Then, when the bankbook was handed back, he checked the entry, put the rubber band around it, and walked next door to Fettucci's grocery and put the bankbook in the cash register, continued on to the storeroom, removed his coat and tie, put on his apron, and went back into the store ready for business. If there was no line at the teller's window, the whole thing didn't take more than five minutes, even passing the time of day.

8. Mr. Hogan was a man who noticed things, and when it came to robbing the bank, this trait stood him in good stead. He had noticed, for instance, where the big bills were kept right in the drawer under the counter, and he had noticed also what days there were likely to be more than other days. Thursday was payday at

the American Can Company's local plant, for instance, so there would be more then. Some Fridays people drew more money to tide them over the weekend. But it was even Steven, maybe not a thousand dollars difference, between Thursdays and Fridays and Saturday mornings. Saturdays were not terribly good because people didn't come to get money that early in the morning, and the bank closed at noon. But he thought it over and came to the conclusion that the Saturday before a long weekend in the summer would be the best of all. People going on trips, vacations, people with relatives visiting, and the bank closed Monday. He thought it out and looked, and sure enough the Saturday morning before Labor Day the cash drawer had twice as much money in it—he saw it when Mr. Cup pulled out the drawer.

9. Mr. Hogan thought about it during all that year, not all the time, of course, but when he had some moments. It was a busy year too. That was the year John and Joan had the mumps and Mrs. Hogan got her teeth pulled and was fitted for a denture. That was the year when Mr. Hogan was Master of the Lodge, with all the time that takes. Larry Shield died that year —he was Mrs. Hogan's brother and was buried from the Hogan house at 215 East Maple. Larry was a bachelor and had a room in the Pine Tree House and he played pool nearly every night. He worked at the Silver Diner but that closed at nine and so Larry would go to Louie's and play pool for an hour. Therefore, it was a surprise when he left enough so that after funeral expenses there were twelve hundred dollars left. And even more surprising that he left a will in Mrs. Hogan's favor, but his double-barreled twelve-gauge shotgun he left to John Hogan, Jr. Mr. Hogan was pleased, although he never hunted. He put the shotgun away in the back of the closet in the bathroom, where he kept his things, to keep it for young John. He didn't want children handling guns and he never bought any shells. It was some of that twelve hundred that got Mrs. Hogan her dentures. Also, she bought a bicycle for John and a doll buggy and walking-talking doll for Joan —a doll with three changes of dresses and a little suit-

case, complete with play make-up. Mr. Hogan thought it might spoil the children, but it didn't seem to. They made just as good marks in school and John even got a job delivering papers. It was a very busy year. Both John and Joan wanted to enter the W. R. Hearst National "I Love America" Contest and Mr. Hogan thought it was almost too much, but they promised to do the work during their summer vacation, so he finally agreed.

10. During that year, no one noticed any difference in Mr. Hogan. It was true, he was thinking about robbing the bank, but he only thought about it in the evening when there was neither a Lodge meeting nor a movie they wanted to go to, so it did not become an obsession and people noticed no change in him.

11. He had studied everything so carefully that the approach of Labor Day did not catch him unprepared or nervous. It was hot that summer and the hot spells were longer than usual. Saturday was the end of two weeks heat without a break and people were irritated with it and anxious to get out of town, although the country was just as hot. They didn't think of that. The children were excited because the "I Love America" Essay Contest was due to be concluded and the winners announced, and the first prize was an all-expense-paid two days trip to Washington, D.C., with every fixing—hotel room, three meals a day, and side trips in a limousine—not only for the winner, but for an accompanying chaperone; visit to the White House —shake hands with the President—everything. Mr. Hogan thought they were getting their hopes too high and he said so.

12. "You've got to be prepared to lose," he told his children. "There're probably thousands and thousands entered. You get your hopes up and it might spoil the whole autumn. Now I don't want any long faces in this house after the contest is over."

13. "I was against it from the start," he told Mrs. Hogan. That was the morning she saw the Washington Monument in her teacup, but she didn't tell anybody about that except Ruth Tyler, Bob Tyler's wife. Ruthie brought over her cards and read them in the Hogan

kitchen, but she didn't find a journey. She did tell Mrs. Hogan that the cards were often wrong. The cards had said Mrs. Winkle was going on a trip to Europe and the next week Mrs. Winkle got a fishbone in her throat and choked to death. Ruthie, just thinking out loud, wondered if there was any connection between the fishbone and the ocean voyage to Europe. "You've got to interpret them right." Ruthie did say she saw money coming to the Hogans.

14. "Oh, I got that already from poor Larry," Mrs. Hogan explained.

15. "I must have got the past and future cards mixed," said Ruthie. "You've got to interpret them right."

16. Saturday dawned a blaster. The early morning weather report on the radio said "Continued hot and humid, light scattered rain Sunday night and Monday." Mrs. Hogan said, "Wouldn't you know? Labor Day." And Mr. Hogan said, "I'm sure glad we didn't plan anything." He finished his egg and mopped the plate with his toast. Mrs. Hogan said, "Did I put coffee on the list?" He took the paper from his handkerchief pocket and consulted it. "Yes, coffee, it's here."

17. "I had a crazy idea I forgot to write it down," said Mrs. Hogan. "Ruth and I are going to Altar Guild this afternoon. It's at Mrs. Alfred Drake's. You know, they just came to town. I can't wait to see their furniture."

18. "They trade with us," said Mr. Hogan. "Opened an account last week. Are the milk bottles ready?"

19. "On the porch."

20. Mr. Hogan looked at his watch just before he picked up the bottles and it was five minutes to eight. He was about to go down the stairs, when he turned and looked back through the opened door at Mrs. Hogan. She said, "Want something, Papa?"

21. "No," he said. "No," and he walked down the steps.

22. He went down to the corner and turned right on Spooner, and Spooner runs into Main Street in two blocks, and right across from where it runs in, there is Fettucci's and the bank around the corner and the

alley beside the bank. Mr. Hogan picked up a handbill in front of Fettucci's and unlocked the door. He went through to the storeroom, opened the door to the alley, and looked out. A cat tried to force its way in, but Mr. Hogan blocked it with his foot and leg and closed the door. He took off his coat and put on his long apron, tied the strings in a bowknot behind his back. Then he got the broom from behind the counter and swept out behind the counters and scooped the sweepings into a dustpan; and, going through the storeroom, he opened the door to the alley. The cat had gone away. He emptied the dustpan into a garbage can and tapped it smartly to dislodge a piece of lettuce leaf. Then he went back to the store and worked for a while on the order sheet. Mrs. Clooney came in for a half a pound of bacon. She said it was hot and Mr. Hogan agreed. "Summers are getting hotter," he said.

23. "I think so myself," said Mrs. Clooney. "How's Mrs. standing up?"

24. "Just fine," said Mr. Hogan. "She's going to Altar Guild."

25. "So am I. I just can't wait to see their furniture," said Mrs. Clooney, and she went out.

26. Mr. Hogan put a five-pound hunk of bacon on the slicer and stripped off the pieces and laid them on wax paper and then he put the wax-paper-covered squares in the cooler cabinet. At ten minutes to nine, Mr. Hogan went to a shelf. He pushed a spaghetti box aside and took down a cereal box, which he emptied in the little closet toilet. Then, with a banana knife, he cut out the Mickey Mouse mask that was on the back. The rest of the box he took to the toilet and tore up the cardboard and flushed it down. He went into the store then and yanked a piece of string loose and tied the ends through the side holes of the mask and then he looked at his watch—a large silver Hamilton with black hands. It was two minutes to nine.

27. Perhaps the next four minutes were his only time of nervousness at all. At one minute to nine, he took the broom and went out to sweep the sidewalk and he swept it very rapidly—was sweeping it, in fact, when Mr. Warner unlocked the bank door. He said

good morning to Mr. Warner and a few seconds later the bank staff of four emerged from the coffee shop. Mr. Hogan saw them across the street and he waved at them and they waved back. He finished the sidewalk and went back in the store. He laid his watch on the little step of the cash register. He sighed very deeply, more like a deep breath than a sigh. He knew that Mr. Warner would have the safe open now and he would be carrying the cash trays to the teller's window. Mr. Hogan looked at the watch on the cash register step. Mr. Kenworthy paused in the store entrance, then shook his head vaguely and walked on and Mr. Hogan let out his breath gradually. His left hand went behind his back and pulled the bowknot on his apron, and then the black hand on his watch crept up on the four-minute mark and covered it.

28. Mr. Hogan opened the charge account drawer and took out the store pistol, a silver-colored Iver Johnson .38. He moved quickly to the storeroom, slipped off his apron, put on his coat, and stuck the revolver in his side pocket. The Mickey Mouse mask he shoved up under his coat where it didn't show. He opened the alley door and looked up and down and stepped quickly out, leaving the door slightly ajar. It is sixty feet to where the alley enters Main Street, and there he paused and looked up and down and then he turned his head toward the center of the street as he passed the bank window. At the bank's swinging door, he took out the mask from under his coat and put it on. Mr. Warner was just entering his office and his back was to the door. The top of Will Cup's head was visible through the teller's grill.

29. Mr. Hogan moved quickly and quietly around the end of the counter and into the teller's cage. He had the revolver in his right hand now. When Will Cup turned his head and saw the revolver, he froze. Mr. Hogan slipped his toe under the trigger of the floor alarm and he motioned Will Cup to the floor with the revolver and Will went down quick. Then Mr. Hogan opened the cash drawer and with two quick movements he piled the large bills from the tray together. He made a whipping motion to Will on the floor, to

indicate that he should turn over and face the wall, and Will did. Then Mr. Hogan stepped back around the counter. At the door of the bank, he took off the mask, and as he passed the window he turned his head toward the middle of the street. He moved into the alley, walked quickly to the storeroom, and entered. The cat had got in. It watched him from a pile of canned goods cartons. Mr. Hogan went to the toilet closet and tore up the mask and flushed it. He took off his coat and put on his apron. He looked out into the store and then moved to the cash register. The revolver went back into the charge account drawer. He punched No Sale and, lifting the top drawer, distributed the stolen money underneath the top tray and then pulled the tray forward and closed the register, and only then did he look at his watch and it was 9:07½.

30. He was trying to get the cat out of the storeroom when the commotion boiled out of the bank. He took his broom and went out on the sidewalk. He heard all about it and offered his opinion when it was asked for. He said he didn't think the fellow could get away—where could he get to? Still, with the holiday coming up—

31. It was an exciting day. Mr. Fettucci was as proud as though it were his bank. The sirens sounded around town for hours. Hundreds of holiday travelers had to stop at the roadblocks set up all around the edge of town and several sneaky-looking men had their cars searched.

32. Mrs. Hogan heard about it over the phone and she dressed earlier than she would have ordinarily and came to the store on her way to Altar Guild. She hoped Mr. Hogan would have seen or heard something new, but he hadn't. "I don't see how the fellow can get away," he said.

33. Mrs. Hogan was so excited, she forgot her own news. She only remembered when she got to Mrs. Drake's house, but she asked permission and phoned the store the first moment she could. "I forgot to tell you. John's won honorable mention."

34. "What?"

35. "In the 'I Love America' Contest."

36. "What did he win?"

37. "Honorable mention."

38. "Fine. Fine—Anything come with it?"

39. "Why, he'll get his picture and his name all over the country. Radio too. Maybe even television. They've already asked for a photograph of him."

40. "Fine," said Mr. Hogan. "I hope it don't spoil him." He put up the receiver and said to Mr. Fettucci, "I guess we've got a celebrity in the family."

41. Fettucci stayed open until nine on Saturdays. Mr. Hogan ate a few snacks from cold cuts, but not much, because Mrs. Hogan always kept his supper warming.

42. It was 9:05, or :06, or :07 when he got back to the brown-shingle house at 215 East Maple. He went in through the front door and out to the kitchen where the family was waiting for him.

43. "Got to wash up," he said, and went up to the bathroom. He turned the key in the bathroom door and then he flushed the toilet and turned on the water in the basin and tub while he counted the money. Eight thousand three hundred and twenty dollars. From the top shelf of the storage closet in the bathroom, he took down the big leather case that held his Knight Templar's uniform. The plumed hat lay there on its form. The white ostrich feather was a little yellow and needed changing. Mr. Hogan lifted out the hat and pried the form up from the bottom of the case. He put the money in the form and then he thought again and removed two bills and shoved them in his side pocket. Then he put the form back over the money and laid the hat on top and closed the case and shoved it back on the top shelf. Finally he washed his hands and turned off the water in the tub and the basin.

44. In the kitchen, Mrs. Hogan and the children faced him, beaming. "Guess what some young man's going on?"

45. "What?" asked Mr. Hogan.

46. "Radio," said John. "Monday night. Eight o'clock."

47. "I guess we got a celebrity in the family," said Mr. Hogan.

48. Mrs. Hogan said, "I just hope some young lady hasn't got her nose out of joint."

49. Mr. Hogan pulled up to the table and stretched his legs. "Mama, I guess I got a fine family," he said. He reached in his pocket and took out two five-dollar bills. He handed one to John. "That's for winning," he said. He poked the other bill at Joan. "And that's for being a good sport. One celebrity and one good sport. What a fine family!" He rubbed his hands together and lifted the lid of the covered dish. "Kidneys," he said. "Fine."

50. And that's how Mr. Hogan did it.

Guide to Analysis

A. SCENES:

1. The first eleven paragraphs are narrated by the teller of the story. Scene One includes paragraph 12 and the first sentences of paragraph 13. Scene Two includes the rest of paragraph 13 and all of 14 and 15. Bracket the twelve scenes which make up this story, and the four transitions. Paragraphs 29 through 41 are again narrated.

2. How much time does this story cover?

3. Offer some good reasons for the extended narrative sections.

4. Order the first eleven paragraphs into tentative scenes. What would each scene contain? Why didn't Steinbeck do this?

5. Why did Steinbeck have Mrs. Hogan forget to tell Mr. Hogan the news and then call him from Mrs. Drake's home (paragraphs 32 through 39)?

6. Make a careful comparison between the scene element content in this story and that in "Sled." Why are Steinbeck's scenes so lacking in the eleven elements, light for instance?

7. Part of Steinbeck's skill with scene derives from his power to suggest strongly the scene elements not reported overtly. Examine Scene Three, for example, and indicate words that suggest scene elements without actually stating them in a report.

8. Would you call these true scenes on our terms?

B. STRUCTURE:

1. Go through the story and indicate all violations of the strictly third person objective point of view. Try to think out why Steinbeck permitted these violations.

2. What effect do these violations have on the story?

3. Can you identify with Hogan? If not, what prevents identification?

4. In Scene Seven, paragraph 7, would it improve the story to omit the sentence: "He knew that Mr. Warner would have the safe open now and he would be carrying the cash trays to the teller's window"? Support your judgment.

5. Place the story on this structural outline:

  I. The causative situation

  II. The deciding character

    a. his governing characteristic:

    b. his problem:

      his first solution:

        the first interference:

      his second solution:

        the intensifications (list all)

  III. The result:

6. Was the result inevitable?

7. Can you find a flaw in the report of Mr. Hogan's procedure?

8. Illustrate Mr. Hogan's obedience to his own dictum: ". . . forget all about hanky-panky."

9. How well does Steinbeck handle panoramic view?

C. DIALOGUE:

1. Steinbeck uses very little dialogue here. In the first narrative passage, what technique substitutes for dialogue, yet has much the same effect as true dialogue?

2. Point out instances of humor in the dialogue.

D. HUMOR:

1. Usually satire has a serious intent, to cause some social action which may lead to improved social mores. Is there any such intent here? Support your argument

2. Analyze one passage which you find humorous. What makes it funny? What is the quality of this humor?

3. Would you call this an important story of similar dimension to "Wullie?"

THE NAMES THAT SPELL
GREAT LITERATURE

Choose from today's most renowned world authors—every one an important addition to your personal library.

Hermann Hesse

☐ 20023	MAGISTER LUDI	$3.50
☐ 20696	DEMIAN	$2.95
☐ 14305	THE JOURNEY TO THE EAST	$2.25
☐ 14956	SIDDHARTHA	$2.75
☐ 14563	BENEATH THE WHEEL	$2.95
☐ 20344	NARCISSUS AND GOLDMUND	$3.25
☐ 14462	STEPPENWOLF	$2.75

Alexander Solzhenitsyn

☐ 20127	THE FIRST CIRCLE	$3.95
☐ 13441	ONE DAY IN THE LIFE OF IVAN DENISOVICH	$2.50
☐ 20655	CANCER WARD	$4.95

Jerzy Kosinski

☐ 14117	STEPS	$2.50
☐ 20554	THE PAINTED BIRD	$3.25
☐ 14952	COCKPIT	$2.75
☐ 14661	BLIND DATE	$2.95
☐ 13843	BEING THERE	$2.50
☐ 14577	THE DEVIL TREE	$2.75

Doris Lessing

☐ 20274	THE SUMMER BEFORE THE DARK	$3.50
☐ 13675	THE GOLDEN NOTEBOOK	$3.95
☐ 13967	THE FOUR-GATED CITY	$3.95
☐ 14398	BRIEFING FOR A DESCENT INTO HELL	$2.95
☐ 20146	MEMOIRS OF A SURVIVOR	$3.50

Buy them at your local bookstore or use this handy coupon for ordering

---

Bantam Books, Inc., Dept. EDG, 414 East Golf Road, Des Plaines, Ill. 60016

Please send me the books I have checked above. I am enclosing $_____ (please add $1.00 to cover postage and handling). Send check or money order —no cash or C.O.D.'s please.

Mr/Mrs/Miss_____

Address_____

City_____State/Zip_____

EDG—10/81

Please allow four to six weeks for delivery. This offer expires 4/82.

READ TOMORROW'S LITERATURE—TODAY

THE BEST OF TODAY'S WRITING BOUND FOR TOMORROW'S CLASSICS.

☐	13545	**SOPHIE'S CHOICE** William Styron	$3.50
☐	14970	**RAGTIME** E. L. Doctorow	$3.50
☐	20274	**THE SUMMER BEFORE THE DARK** Doris Lessing	$3.50
☐	13441	**ONE DAY IN THE LIFE OF IVAN DENISOVICH** Alexander Solzhenitsyn	$2.50
☐	20178	**THE END OF THE ROAD** John Barth	$3.50
☐	13675	**THE GOLDEN NOTEBOOK** Doris Lessing	$3.95
☐	20146	**MEMOIRS OF A SURVIVOR** Doris Lessing	$3.50
☐	13888	**THE CRYING OF LOT 49** Thomas Pynchon	$2.75
☐	14761	**GRAVITY'S RAINBOW** Thomas Pynchon	$4.95
☐	20580	**EVEN COWGIRLS GET THE BLUES** Tom Robbins	$3.95
☐	01260	**STILL LIFE WITH WOODPECKER** Tom Robbins	$6.95
☐	14373	**BURR** Gore Vidal	$3.50
☐	13843	**BEING THERE** Jerzy Kosinski	$2.50
☐	20332	**V** Thomas Pynchon	$3.95
☐	20554	**THE PAINTED BIRD** Jerzy Kosinski	$3.25

Buy them at your local bookstore or use this handy coupon for ordering:

START A COLLECTION

With Bantam's fiction anthologies, you can begin almost anywhere. Choose from science fiction, classic litera- by both new and established writers in America and ture, modern short stories, mythology, and more—all around the world.